Powerful Schools

How schools can be drivers of social and global mobility

Dr Helen Wright

A John Catt Publication

First Published 2016

by John Catt Educational Ltd,
12 Deben Mill Business Centre, Old Maltings Approach,
Melton, Woodbridge IP12 1BL

Tel: +44 (0) 1394 389850 Fax: +44 (0) 1394 386893
Email: enquiries@johncatt.com
Website: www.johncatt.com

ISBN: 978 1 909717 84 8

Set and designed by John Catt Educational Limited

Social mobility is one of the great challenges of our age and Helen's rallying cry to those who work in schools is both powerful and timely. Her work does not simply outline a philosophy; it provides clear guidance on how to deliver the required changes and sets a challenge to educators everywhere to create 'Powerful Schools'.

Kevin Fear, Headmaster, Nottingham High School

Compelling and aspirational, Helen argues with great conviction and energy that schools are powerful hubs of social change and that if teachers and school leaders are committed to facilitating the choices of the students in their care they can drive social and global mobility.

Jill Berry, educational consultant, author, former state and independent school Head

Helen convinced me that her suggestions would make a significant positive contribution to the improvement of equal opportunities. Definitely a book in my back-pack!

Dr. Neil Hawkes, Founder of the International Values-based Trust (IVET)

Chapter 7, in particular, is really excellent: powerful, detailed and practical; it is also unusual, in the number and breadth of its ideas.

Baroness Shephard of Northwold, Secretary of State for Education and Employment, 1995-1997. Deputy Chair of the Social Mobility and Child Poverty Commission, chair of the Council of the Institute of Education until 2015.

Dr Helen Wright

Dr Helen Wright is a leading commentator on education and a well-known school principal, leading schools in the UK and Australia for over 13 years. Since 2014 she has been deeply involved in developing new international schools in regions across the globe, as a Founding Partner in Global Thought Leadership.

Her international experience combines with her incisive focus on education to form a vision of the transformative power of education for all – locally, nationally and globally. In everything she does, Oxford-educated Dr Wright believes firmly and unwaveringly in the power of human beings – especially our young people – to make a positive difference and to change the world for the better.

She is a non-executive director and advisory board member on a number of boards in the UK and overseas, including two education technology start-ups. Most importantly, she derives great joy from inspiring individuals and organisations to create original and innovative strategic and practical solutions to challenging problems.

www.linkedin.com/in/drhelenwright
www.globalthought.co.uk

Contents

Foreword

Vision, inspiration and passion are characteristics of this also eminently practical book. Dr Helen Wright provides all educators with a guide to the opportunities we can make available for our students, the future generations of our world. The teaching profession, not always appropriately valued by developed societies, has enormous responsibilities inherent in its nature and role.

The United Kingdom is fortunate in having one of the most admired education systems in the world. Globally there are over 5000 international schools in non-English speaking countries using English as a medium of instruction. Of these, the largest group follows the English curriculum and teaches for British examinations. 'British' is synonymous with 'quality'. This small country is punching above its weight educationally. It therefore has enormous opportunities to help not only its own students, but also educational systems throughout the world.

Education has traditionally facilitated social mobility and to this we can now add as well increasing global mobility. It is difficult for teachers to envisage what our fast changing world will be like in one or two generations, or indeed what kind of work will be available for today' s children. But teachers have to try to educate for that unknown world. Dr Wright's book is an invaluable help to open our minds and broaden our horizons. Her experience as a prestigious educator in the UK and abroad has given her a unique understanding of education globally and the impact it has on future generations and on the future of the world itself.

As the Nobel Peace Prize Laureate Nelson Mandela said, "Education is the most powerful weapon you can use to change the world".

School leaders have the opportunity to inspire all those around them, especially the stakeholders in their schools, enabling them to become aware of the opportunities open to their students in social and global mobility. It is easier now than ever before, with modern communications such as internet and mass travel, to translate such aspirations into actions. Local, national and international communities are developing networks as never before.

It is not often that we are treated to a book that includes both theory and practice, but here we have one. School leaders and teachers everywhere will find a mine of information, as well as practical suggestions, for applying the powerful ideas that this book brings us.

Sir Roger Fry CBE,
Chairman, King's Group
March 2016

Introduction

Mobility (n): The ability to move or be moved freely and easily

Social mobility (n): The ability to move freely between different levels in society or employment

Global mobility (n): The ability to move freely around the world to live and work internationally and/or in different cultures

This book is about how schools really could change the world, starting tomorrow.

In a sense, it is a book for everyone who has any interest at all in the power of education to make a difference. It is of particular and practical interest, however, to current and aspiring teachers and school leaders.

Schools are tremendous powerhouses. They have social legitimacy globally: most children across most of the world spend a significant proportion of their waking hours in direct contact with schools between the ages of around 4 and 18. Schools therefore have an amazing opportunity – and obligation – to influence and improve the lives of young people who are the adults of the future. They recognise this: great school leaders will eulogise about this moral imperative, and will transform it into action and practice in their schools.

And yet there is more – which again, school leaders recognise and drive forward. Schools help shape individuals in order to prepare them for citizenship in society, and it follows logically that they have the capacity to shape individuals in order that they will use their citizenship to help create a better society. In 'economic speak', schools are prime generators of human capital and therefore wealth, and they therefore have the potential to be the principal engines of social mobility and global mobility in the world. We often view schools largely as preparatory institutions, helping children to make the transition to adulthood by preparing them to take examinations (and also develop skills) which will allow them to go on to further study or work; the concept of Powerful Schools as explored in this book is about how schools are so much more than this, and how they can – and should – be central, powerful hubs of social change.

Leaders of schools from Nursery to Primary and Secondary stages already know and recognise, keenly, that they have a key and a privileged role in the lives of young people, and they are strongly motivated to make the best choices for them, in order to help them grow into the rounded young adults that they can be. They know that much is expected of them, and that it is nigh on impossible to do everything they could do for young people within the time that they have, the curriculum and regulatory frameworks within which they work, and their own capabilities and the support they receive. People outside schools rarely know just how much work and energy goes on inside schools to help young people grow and develop.

And yet all educators know deep down that if we could re-orientate schools just a little so that they sat firmly at the centre of society – well-funded, well-respected, well-recognised, and unequivocally trusted to try out innovative and far-reaching solutions – then there is so much more that could be done within the scope of their roles. If educators are liberated to recognise that this potential of schools – this power – need not be constrained by expectations about qualifications, curriculum, age limits, the length of the school day, or the physical buildings which the school inhabits, then their imagination soars, as does their capacity for invention. Just think what schools could achieve if school leaders were empowered and enabled to draw on whatever resources they needed; just think what a difference schools could help make in the world.

One of the most powerful resources that teachers and school leaders have at their disposal is their creative vision, based on their deep knowledge of young people and their professional awareness of what can make a difference to the life chances of their students. This book seeks to release this creative vision. It is about how schools can lead the way in establishing structures and practices that will support all young people to become productive members of a global society.

It is not a treatise for revolution in schools or a call to dismantle existing curricula and structures – for the most part, anyway, that is unnecessary. It does not cover every aspect of how to run a school, or what a school is for. Rather, it focuses in on one crucial element that has always underpinned the development of universal schooling, and yet which we could and should still do better: social mobility, and its increasingly important cousin, global mobility. Together, social and global mobility are major drivers in developing schooling and education systems across the world: schools have it within their power to make equal opportunity possible. Greater social and global mobility result in fundamentally more equal opportunities, and schools can be powerful catalysts for this.

This is a book that takes a pragmatic approach, focusing on the practical action that schools can take themselves in order genuinely to lead a drive that will create far greater opportunities for social and global mobility for all. This book attempts to inspire and to act as a stimulus for action, not to preach. It recognises how much schools are already doing in this arena, while challenging them to do even more. Its ultimate goal is to help each and every school to grow abundantly rich in opportunities for individuals to develop the skills to become more socially and globally mobile, actively supported by numerous people and organisations who are consciously working to engage them in making the most of these opportunities.

It is not a book that looks at every possible aspect of school development. It focuses on a single and very specific – although also arguably utterly fundamental – part of what schools do, and it looks in detail at how schools can stretch themselves to develop still further what they are innately doing to improve the social and global mobility of the young people for whose education they have responsibility. Some schools will have other, more urgent priorities, yet even these schools, beset perhaps with demands to address identified failures or to meet new regulatory requirements, should consider how a drive towards greater social and global mobility could become a focal point for general improvement on which all the school's activity could converge.

Chapter 1 examines what we mean by social and global mobility, why it is important, and why schools should be leading the drive to develop it. Chapter 2 explores the potential influence and impact of schools, and how schools can extend their influence. It paints a picture of what powerful schools could look like in practice. Chapter 3 looks at the major stakeholders in school, as a starting point for thinking about who schools can engage in their strategy. Chapter 4 discusses in detail how schools can plan for change, and what they need to consider internally to make this effective. Chapter 5 considers why a school's stakeholders might be motivated to contribute to a vision of Powerful Schools, together with insights into what they might contribute. Chapter 6 sets out different approaches that schools can take to engage their stakeholders, and Chapter 7 – by far the longest chapter – is rich with practical ideas for action. Chapter 8 – the conclusion – is short and to the point: all that is needed now is action.

The central emphasis of this book is on what schools can do – starting now, and in the medium and long term – to develop the social and global mobility of their students. It explains why this is so important, both for individuals and for society itself. The premise of this book unequivocally places schools at the centre of society, and calls on school leaders to take on the mantle of responsibility for social and global mobility in, among and beyond their schools. It has been written to help school leaders and teachers free their thinking, flex their muscles, and begin to translate the vision of Powerful Schools into a practical manifestation. This book shows them how.

Chapter 1

Mobility, Power and Schools: why are they important?

Why mobility matters

Social mobility

The definition of 'society' in this book is deliberately open, because the ideas and practical suggestions are designed to work well in a wide range of contexts, and can and should be adapted to these contexts. Inevitably, however, given the origins of the book in a developed English-speaking Western country, the concept of society embedded within this book is heavily influenced by Western philosophy and Western ideas about equality, respect (for the individual and for society) and freedom of thought. Society is more than simply a collection of people – it is a structured or semi-structured collective, in which people are supported and enabled to do more together than they are able to do alone. It is possible to debate at length the precise nature of the ideals and beliefs underpinning our broad and shared understandings of society, for one of the great influences on modern Western thought was the 18th century Enlightenment, which actively encouraged reasoning; this book, however, is about practical action, and school leaders will very quickly discern whether or not the underlying principles it contains resonate with their own understandings of how society can and should function.

The drive towards freedom embedded in this understanding of society – freedom of self, of others, of thought, and so on – is one of the main reasons why social mobility has such significance as a concept, and why it is worth devoting time to working out how to develop it. Social mobility is essentially about the freedom of movement within a society, so that people are not defined or limited by the income or social status of their parents or families. Action designed to improve social mobility is not simply about making it possible for more people to earn more money, however – it is about creating opportunities for people (or enabling them to create their own opportunities) so that they are able to choose how to live their lives, including the roles they decide to take on and where they decide to live and work. To a certain extent, knowledge is power in this respect – to become socially mobile, people need to learn about potential pathways ahead of them that can take them in different directions, and they need to learn too about how to embark on and follow these pathways. In many cases, though, and especially as our society has come relatively recently to the concept of universal equality, and so is still working on this, these pathways do not yet exist, or are still particularly difficult to access. In these cases, knowledge is not sufficient, but rather work needs to be done to forge the pathways themselves. Knowledge and action in combination will make a difference to the social mobility of our society.

Global mobility
In practice, in our technologically connected world, and where international travel is easier than it has ever been, social and global mobility are intertwined. Global mobility as understood in this book is not about the ability to take holidays overseas; rather, it is about extending the cultural and practical awareness of people so that they can learn about, and learn to respect, different cultures across the world, and so that they are better enabled to live and work in them. Global mobility is intrinsic to social mobility: when people are enabled to move freely around the world, and to feel comfortable living and working in different countries, then they reach a new level of freedom of choice.

Global mobility can therefore perhaps be seen as a subdivision of social mobility, and it is essential if people are to be able to choose to move freely within our global world. It does not mean that by enabling young people to be globally mobile we are requiring them to live and work abroad for some or all of their lifetime; it does mean, however, that we are empowering them to be able to choose to live and work abroad. Social mobility is all about facilitating choices, and exactly the same applies to global mobility.

Enabling and supporting global mobility for everyone brings its own particular challenges for individuals and for schools, of course: it is still a relatively new concept, and as such there is much more work to be done to conceptualise the pathways that need to be created in order to make it possible. Distance is a big issue – not just the physical distance that exists between different countries and continents (which effectively rules out teaching about the practicalities of other cultures on a series of day trips), but also the distance that can exist between different cultures and our own. Just as geographical difference is magnified when we talk about global mobility, so too are other differences – cultural, linguistic, social, philosophical. All of these make the development of global mobility a greater challenge, but no less a crucial one: again, in a world which has actively sought for decades to develop a shared rule of law through the United Nations, and where people can now connect very easily around the world through technology – in nano-seconds, in fact – and where the strength and quality of these connections are growing daily, to the extent that people already have an understanding, however basic and unrefined, of global society, then if young people are not actively made to appreciate the world in this way and to prepare for it, they will miss out on significant opportunities. In effect, their social mobility will be limited.

Preparing for global mobility is therefore, arguably, an essential component of social mobility, and should form part of any drive in schools towards greater social mobility. Teaching about global mobility has another, equally positive consequence: greater understanding can lead to greater tolerance of others and, in due course, we can hope, a greater likelihood of more harmonious co-existence within and among groups of people across the world. Idealism is a powerful driver in education.

Schools have the ability to make a difference

Schools seek to make a difference, with a desire of creating a better world for all, and they have the ability to do so. Sometimes, caught up as we can be in the day-to-day demands of school life, we need to be reminded that education is a fundamental bedrock of our society. Education is embedded into global society as a human right: Article 26 of the 1948 Universal Declaration of Human Rights states clearly and unambiguously that "everyone has the right to education". The commitment of the UN to 'Education for All', which tied in with the UN's Millennium Development Goals agreed in 2000, was based on the concept of education not only as a 'right', but as a "passport to human development … It opens doors and expands opportunities and freedoms. It contributes to fostering peace, democracy and economic growth as well as improving health and reducing poverty."

With the advent of the UN's Sustainable Development Goals in late 2015, the UN has developed this concept further in its drives towards 'Education 2030', which encompasses Goal 4 of the UN Sustainable Development Goals: "Ensure inclusive and quality education for all and promote lifelong learning". This goal firmly commits governments to enabling equality of access to education for all, and a focus on education at all levels "leading to relevant and effective learning outcomes". Equality, relevance and effectiveness at an individual, local, national and global level: these three key aims are all supported by, and are intrinsic to, drives to develop social and global mobility in our world, and specifically for our young people. The measure of equality in a globally connected world is not only a comparison with one's immediate neighbour, but with people around the world, and an education which is relevant and effective will prepare children and young people to be able to work globally as well as locally. This does not mean that all children and young people must be expected or required to live and work abroad, nor that they should all be prepared for the same careers and ways of life. Valuing individuality and difference is actually a crucial part of enabling true equality. It does mean, however, that all children and young people need to be given similar opportunities to grow, develop and prepare for life in a global world. Although these opportunities may have to be tailored to different circumstances and to the differing needs of individuals, they nonetheless must lead to a similar, overarching outcome, namely that young people are genuinely enabled to choose what to do with their lives. This choice is at the heart of true social and global mobility. An education which is truly relevant and effective will also, in the context of education as a driver of social change, almost certainly prepare young people to challenge inequality and to seek to create even greater opportunities and expectations of social and global mobility for future generations.

There is of course an ethical complexity that lies at the heart of such a drive: who are we, school leaders may ask, to help guide young people, expectantly, towards a future in which the choices that underpin social and global mobility are far from universally in place, and may even – as yet – be beyond their reach? How do we know that the change that we are promoting will be beneficial to our students? In focusing on social and global mobility, are we doing the right thing for our students, or are we setting them up for potential disappointment and failure?

School leaders who worry about this ethical complexity can take heart from the very fact that they are asking these questions and that they are seeking answers. Education is all about change, and often deals with the unknown; the ethics of education are therefore highly complex. At the very least, however, if we are aware of this and actively reflect on these issues, collectively, then we are far more likely to make choices and decisions which will, ultimately, help young people grow into adults who have more opportunities, and more choices. The UN's Education 2030 treatise is explicit in recognising that this is an age of "change, complexity and paradox", and yet – hearteningly – it does not hold back from driving forward: "The complexity of today's world requires a comprehensive approach to education policy embedded in a better understanding of the way in which knowledge is created, controlled, disseminated, acquired, validated and used. It also requires further development of the ethical principles that govern education and knowledge as common goods."

There is no tried and tested roadmap for education as a means to social and global mobility. In time, we can hope that one will exist – when, eventually, we get to a point where we can genuinely say that every child, worldwide, has equal opportunities in life, and we have worked out what to do in order to make this happen, so that we can replicate it for future generations. Up until this point, when school leaders engage actively with the ideas of social and global mobility, they are taking on some of the responsibility themselves for drawing the roadmap, and with this comes an enormous ethical responsibility too.

School leaders already embrace this ethical responsibility, however. Many school leaders would argue that they have always seen social and global mobility as implicitly (even explicitly) central to what happens in schools, and they would naturally observe too that everything that schools do already contributes to such mobility. They are right, of course – any and all education makes a difference to children's opportunities in life – but even the school leaders for whom social mobility and global mobility come explicitly high up the reasons why they do what they do in schools can still extend their reach further, by:

- becoming clearer themselves about why social and global mobility are so important, and what this might look like in practice;

- evaluating how their own school or schools actively contribute to social and global mobility, not just of the students in their care, but also of society and the world community in general;

- developing programmes in school to sharpen awareness of social and global mobility amongst all the stakeholders in schools;

- developing programmes in school that will engage as many people as possible, from a wide range of sectors beyond the school, in practical action; and

- contributing – through developing best practice, influencing and engaging – to the global debate and movement around fleshing out the ethical principles and practices underpinning universal education to which the international community has committed, to ensure that social and global mobility are appropriately recognised.

Effective social and global mobility is an aspirational vision, and it should sit firmly within the remit of schools because schools are licensed and explicitly empowered by society – at a global as well as local and national level – to prepare young people for a role in society, both as individuals and as citizens. A driving force in human societies is to create a better society; schools are charged with educating the children and young people in our society, and preparing them – collectively, over and above their individual and very varied preparation within their own families – for their future as individuals and as members of society. Schools have a key and uniquely privileged opportunity to help develop social and global mobility, and they operate within a social framework which can endorse this drive, and enable and empower schools to pursue it.

What gets in the way?

Powerful schools can make an enormous difference to the social and global mobility of their students … and yet, realistically, much gets in the way of the work of schools in this respect:

The complexity of schools

Schools are intensely complex places. The myriad of growing and changing personalities, the wide range of emotions in play, the spectrum of relationships on show: the impact of all of these, brought together in a single place, is vast. Schools are not stable, easily manageable places: they deal with human beings who are changing and growing rapidly, who have not reached physical, emotional, cognitive and social maturity, and the role of schools is to play a major role in enabling them to achieve these goals. The deliberate focus of schools is to prompt change, and the very nature of education and personal growth means that a school will be different every day, because if it is doing its job properly, each of the individual young people within it will have been changed, even if almost imperceptibly, through their experiences the previous day. This change and growth can happen as a result of experiences that they have had not just in school but at home, or outside the home; school, however, is a focal point for the moulding of this experience. Schools are not neat, uncomplicated places, and it often comes as a surprise to people who enter schools from outside the education sector just how complex the management of schools can be.

Primal emotions run high in schools, in ways which they do not in other organisations. Parents can be hugely invested in schools, which brings negatives as well as positives, and sometimes reactions are – entirely understandably – emotional rather than rational. Add to this volatile mix the management of the adults employed in schools, and the staffing and resourcing structures which they bring, and the complexity deepens. These issues are similar to those found in any other organisation – which, as many CEOs or HR Directors will freely admit, are challenging enough to manage in their own right. Add further the swathes of regulatory and budgetary requirements to which schools are subject, then it is unsurprising that a common (and eminently reasonable) complaint of anyone who works in school is that there simply isn't enough time – and there aren't enough people – to do everything.

Public perceptions of schools

It is a curious phenomenon that the more developed a society, the less valued its schools seem to be. In societies where education is not universal, it is often highly prized, and schools are seen as places which make a radical difference to young people's lives. In societies where universal education is compulsory, it appears often to be taken for granted and as a result is often not prized to the same extent. Couple this with a 21st century media-driven culture which values soundbites and sensationalism, and it is easy to see why the complexities of education do not translate well into easy communication, and why there are often more stories circulating about what is wrong with teachers and schools than about what is right.

There are probably a number of other reasons for the lower value attached to schools in developed societies. Part of it is no doubt down to a general social complacency about living and working standards which forgets that education has underpinned (and continues to underpin) all the developments which make our society safe and desirable; part of it is also probably down to the fact that most adults really do not know what goes on in schools today, as compared to schools when they came through the education system. Many school buildings have remained the same externally for hundreds of years; what goes on inside the walls, however, has expanded dramatically during that time. Over the years, schools and teachers have not necessarily prioritised keeping the rest of society informed about their professional workings – even parents of children in the school are often not exposed to the details of how schools work, although they see the outcomes and achievements. As many a school leader will remark, misinformed criticism is rife.

It is very easy to see why schools have not spent time on what might effectively be seen to be a public relations drive about their purpose and their central power in society – such a drive could easily have diverted valuable resources (including time as well as money) from the core activity of schools in developing young people who attend the school each day. Besides, schools which are part of a wider, state-sponsored system do not have an imperative to prove their worth in order to recruit students, as they will be provided with a steady flow of children. Even when parents have a choice of schools, their focus is usually primarily on whether the school they choose will provide a happy and successful experience for their child, not on whether schools have a social value in themselves.

Schools are often closed institutions, and while this is in some degree down to a fear (regrettably, a real fear) about the safety and security of the children in their care, it has had a deleterious effect on how schools are perceived. It is unfortunately the case that decades of not making the case for the power of schools have probably contributed to a decline in a general public understanding of the value of schools, and therefore also resulted in a situation where it is increasingly difficult to recruit teachers and school leaders. If young people leaving school do not see the wider value of schools and are not inspired by this, and they are not prompted by positive messages in the society around them about education and its attractiveness as a career, then it is little surprise that they do not opt to train as teachers.

Interestingly, schools which need to communicate effectively with the outside world and prove their worth in order to attract students – schools, often fee-paying, which depend on parental income, which are generally independent of state systems, and which focus to a much greater degree on building an attractive public profile – are usually much more effective at recruiting teachers too. People are attracted by the success of schools, but they need to have this picture of success actively painted for them.

Primarily, of course, the crux of the matter is that people do not realise that schools generate significant wealth. If they think about them at all in economic terms, they see schools as cost centres rather than as profit-generating centres – albeit worthy and necessary cost centres. The thought lingers that schools cost too much, and that they do not contribute back financially to the wider economy. This could not be further from the truth, and perhaps it might take an economic argument to help re-orientate public perception of schools. Schools have powerful local economies – they employ hundreds of people, who plough their earnings into the national GDP and who need and use local services. Schools use a range of services themselves, including construction, catering and cleaning. They also provide employment for government and associated organisations which check what is going on in schools and measure it against externally-verified standards.

Most importantly of all, however, they develop the human capital – the young people – who will work, lead, invent and develop the economy of the future. Schools are not the only places where people learn, as the success stories of entrepreneurs who have 'failed' at school appear to demonstrate, but these stories are unusual and do not always delve into the impact that school has had on their story. Sometimes, a reaction to or rejection of school is a strong prompt for success; without the presence of schools, would the entrepreneur have been as successful?

We can't know this for certain, but we do know that anything that has ever been created or invented is underpinned by learning, and we also know that for the majority of young people, school is where they learn much that they don't learn elsewhere, and where they are enabled to understand the world better, and to function in it. Without schools, or some kind of organised learning, wealth creation would be a lot harder, as well as a lot less equitable. Without schools, arguably our economy would decline and potentially even collapse – and not nearly enough attention is paid to this powerful role that schools have.

Everything else that schools have to do

Schools are incredibly busy places already – they have a full-on job as it is. They help keep children safe, and they take them through nationally agreed pathways of curriculum programmes that give them an introduction to fundamental knowledge about the world and the skills to use this knowledge. They prepare them to sit national examinations. They communicate with parents and carers, and they report frequently and extensively to local and national bodies which oversee their activity, and which check that schools are adhering to the many regulations to which they are subjected. They often work with numerous external agencies to help particularly challenged young people.

Moreover, schools run programmes to develop the personal and social skills of their students, they run clubs and activities to extend their interest, and they help develop the whole person through exposure to physical activity, music, drama and art. They prepare them to some extent for the workplace through programmes of work experience. They help them apply for higher education places. They give them leadership roles in school. They encourage community service. They are demanding, tiring places to work in, which are always seeking to improve. A major hurdle for schools in seeking to do more, or to focus or deepen their existing activity, is their lack of capacity to introduce new initiatives while managing all that they are already doing.

So ...When schools are so busy, why add social and global mobility into the mix?

Given all of these elements, it is entirely understandable why it is very easy for schools to become inward-looking and reluctant to add to what they do, racing as they are to manage what they are tasked to do currently, and to keep up with the everyday demands placed upon them. The thought of reaching out and seeking to reorientate the school so that it does something different, and plays a different role in the eyes of society – particularly in a society which is all too quick to criticise schools – can be a daunting one for school leaders, especially if they think they are doing this by themselves, and within the limitations they have of time, space, people and resources. Besides, they know that what they are doing anyway is already making a difference to the lives of individual young people, and to groups of young people. Why do more?

This is a very valid question. It has answers, however:

- Schools have a fundamental moral obligation to enable equal opportunities for all, and in the 21st century, one of these opportunities revolves around mobility – social and global.

- Schools are already part of the way along the road. This is not a new or radical departure for them: schools are already contributing significantly to social and global mobility – and once they identify what they are already doing, the main thrust of this book is that a few simple steps will help them to reorientate their vision to give a prominence to this social and global mobility and to extend their reach in this respect. The scope of what they might do at a later stage, and the effects they might have are consequently larger, and these choices will be encouraged throughout this book, but if every school took even a few basic, easy steps, they could make a significant difference.

- Schools are the prime engine of change in our society. They are powerhouses, and society (and the world) benefits when we all recognise this and empower them: schools are and should be powerful. Powerful Schools make a difference, and school leaders – working in schools every day – are at the heart of this engine. They are the obvious choice to make change happen.

A powerful vision can harness the complexity of schools, because it can allow people to connect with a core idea and yet interpret it – and act on it – differently, thereby reaching out more effectively into the wider world. A powerful vision can and should shift public perceptions of schools so that they are recognised as the valuable powerhouses that they are and can be. Schools – and their leaders – can do this.

Closing the attainment gap

This vision of change for social equality is important: developing social and global mobility can make a significant difference in closing what is usually termed 'the attainment gap' – the difference between how children from less wealthy families achieve in society compared to the children of more affluent families. This attainment gap is clearly identified and increasingly carefully tracked in societies which wrestle with the fact that although their core values stress equality of access to opportunity, success in this respect is harder to come by for children from poorer backgrounds. The focus of most interventions is on academic skills – literacy and numeracy – and these are increasingly tracked in extensive assessment regimes from an early age. This focus is understandable, because success in national examinations increases choices at further and higher education levels, and these examinations are in many cases a gateway to jobs and careers: the more successful a child is in examinations, the more options he or she has in the future.

However, focusing on academic qualifications as a means to enable social mobility is limited in its effectiveness, particularly as national examinations often have constraints built into them that restrict the number of students who are able to achieve top grades. This is sometimes a reaction to fears that national or state examinations are becoming easier, or that there is 'grade inflation', and this means, effectively, that the aim of all students achieving, equally, the highest grades is effectively unattainable. This has a limiting effect on the impact of academic qualifications to promote social and global mobility. Moreover, repeated testing of children has yet to reveal itself to be truly desirable, and many teachers would comment that it comes with many negative corollaries, including heightened student anxiety and less time to spend on learning in schools. More examinations are not going to be the answer to social and global mobility.

A focus on national examinations as the answer to social mobility also overlooks the importance of global mobility as a powerful prompt to greater social mobility. Global mobility has yet to enter the policy debate in a systematic way, yet, as explored earlier in this chapter, there is an immense value to concentrating some effort on global mobility. Developing the ability of young people to compete globally, and to feel comfortable living and working in and with other cultures, will enlarge their horizons and increase their future opportunities. This is social mobility in action in the uber-connected world of the 21st century.

Better exam results are not the single solution to inequality in social and global mobility. This is recognised in a report by the UK Social Mobility and Child Poverty Commission, published in 2014: 'Cracking the code: how schools can improve social mobility'. Although the authors of the report argue robustly for the prime importance of a focus in schools on academic attainment in order to enable social mobility, they also stress that other elements are important too: "The chances of doing well in a job are not determined solely by academic success – the possession of character skills like persistence and 'grit' also matter. So too do wider opportunities, including work experience, extra-curricular activities and careers advice." (p i).

The fifth of the report's five 'code-breakers', *ie* actions that can and will make a difference to the social mobility of young people, is explicit in its wider focus: "Preparing students for all aspects of life not just for exams – this means supporting children's social and emotional development and the character skills that underpin learning. It also means working with students to identify career goals early and providing excellent careers advice, treating extracurricular activities as key to the school experience and – particularly in secondary schools – encouraging a strong focus on working with business and universities, not – as in some schools – treating these things as optional extras." (p viii). Schools can do more to support social and global mobility than just prepare students effectively for exams.

Not necessarily easy, but worth it

While a few easy steps can make a huge difference to individuals, there is no point in trying to pretend that pursuing a greater, stronger vision of the role of schools in enabling social and global mobility will be a straightforward or even linear process. In its basic form, of course, it is, because schools could just keep doing what they are already doing, and they will still continue to have an impact. A more ambitious approach to developing social and global mobility much, much further is going to be more challenging. Most things that are worth doing in life, of course, are rarely easy. School leaders should not be put off by this, though – rather, they should be energised by it. As the authors of the 2014 report into social mobility in schools recognise, society needs to be spurred into action: social mobility "needs a collective effort from government, parents, employers and educators among others." (p ii). Someone needs to take a lead on it, however. A few extra actions taken in schools could help make a fundamental shift in how people understand schools and in how members of society – as individuals, organisations, businesses and policy-makers – interact with, and invest in, our schools. This is a powerful vision.

Effective change requires strong leadership. The engine of a car does not always start first time: it may need to be nudged into action, and the ignition key may need to be turned a number of times before the engine starts turning over. Without the driver turning the key, the car – no matter how smart, polished, well-oiled or ready to get on the road – will never get going. And without the driver, the car will not go either – no matter how important the people gathered around it. In this analogy, school leaders are the drivers: they are in schools every day. They know their schools and they have the power to make a difference: to start the car and then drive it. Together they are stronger, of course, and this potential for collaboration will be explored later. Personal reflection is a good starting point – a precursor to understanding the vision, communicating it to others, and engaging them in planned action – and so the next part of this book focuses on what Powerful Schools could look like in practice.

First, though, a word on 'power' and education

Power gets a bad rap – and, it must be said, with good reason. Abuse of power has been rife throughout history by governments, organisations and individuals. It is arguably the case that the more power any individual or institution has, the less likely it is to wield that power well; we are ever mindful of the words of the English historian Lord Acton:

> *"Power tends to corrupt and absolute power corrupts absolutely."*

And yet, education – nominally 'a good thing' – can be seen as being all about power. Schools are invested with authority by the social system in which they operate, and education is a powerful process: it seeks to unlock awareness and understanding, develop skills, and open doors so that young people have more opportunities. The power of the teacher or school leader in influencing and changing young people is enormous. To avoid the inhibiting conclusion that we cannot allow schools to become more powerful, for fear that they will somehow turn into tyrants, we have to remind ourselves that power of itself is not the issue; it is the wielding of the power that has the potential to harm, and this is why it is crucial that the three main thrusts of education are equally weighted:

- the development of the individual and his/her uniqueness
- the development in the individual of the sense of belonging to

society, and the value of interaction and collaboration
- the development of the core value of respect for others and the world, and – crucially – of critical reflection and judgement.

What is best for society and what is best for the individual may or may not coincide; it is the third element of critical reflection – and of scepticism in its broadest sense – which helps individuals find an equilibrium in their thinking and their actions. This is also the element that helps keep educators on track in their attempt to ensure that they do what is best for all. Critical reflection is essential: while opposition and criticism of one's ideas may not always be immediately welcome, they are an intrinsic part of our thoughtful interaction with other individuals, and help us both to articulate our beliefs and to adapt them as we seek to engage others in them. Constant reflection about why, as well as how, schools can and should become more powerful is a central – and balancing – feature of this book, as it should be of any process which leads to change in schools.

Given the cognitive as well as the practical effort involved, it is easy to want to shy away from repositioning schools so that they have more power in society, as this book seeks to do. How, after all, can we know that what we are doing as school leaders is right? In truth, we can't – but we can have a pretty good guess, using our accumulated professional experience and wisdom, our belief in the power of education, and the skills of critical reflection that we have personally and collectively developed through careers in education, together with the voices and opinions of others, to help us question continuously and test and evaluate our proposed solutions. We have to come to a position of understanding which we are prepared to maintain, even in the face of opposition, while retaining an openness to other opinions and perspectives. To put it simply, though, we have to believe enough that what we are doing is right enough for us to get out of bed in the morning without suffering an existentialist crisis.

A fear of power may ultimately disempower us, and we need to get beyond this hurdle. In order to help effect positive change in a world where we are all still seeking, and looking to create, answers to poverty, injustice, unhappiness and lack of freedom, and where we believe that education has a vital role to play in solving all of these, then all we can realistically do is to be as well-motivated, as thoughtful, and as active as possible. 'Doing our best' is probably as good as it can get – and if by doing our best we can make a positive difference to young people and, ideally, to the world in general, we can take heart from this.

Chapter 2

Dimensions of Powerful Schools: what does Powerful look like in practice?

Easy wins

Doing <u>something</u> to develop social and global mobility is really easy. All schools need to do is:

- enable their students to believe (even just a little bit more than they do to start with) that they can move freely in life and in the world – ie, essentially, that they can do anything that they set their mind to.

- give their students some opportunities to develop some of the practical experience and skills that they will need to be able to move freely in life and in the world (*eg* help in gaining qualifications which will give them choices at the next stage of their life, work experience, opportunities to hear and interact with people who can introduce them to aspects of life after school, opportunities to visit other countries).

Your school is probably doing this already. In fact, it is probably accurate to say that all schools are contributing something valuable to social and global mobility, just by continuing to do what they do at present. They can congratulate themselves on this, and – if they choose to – they can just keep doing what they are doing. It will certainly help develop the social and global mobility of their students.

But there is much, much more that schools can do. They can seek to better what they are already doing – and can draw on research and evidence about best practice in schools that will help them strengthen the impact and outcomes of their current activity. They can also think ambitiously and creatively about how they can take a leap forward – and help society more broadly take a leap forward – into developing social and global mobility for all. They can take the lead on this social movement. Schools can do much more to lead to a future transformation in social and global mobility.

Taking the lead on social and global mobility involves creating a comprehensive, ambitious and bold vision for schools. Imagine:

- a school where young people leave at the age of 18 with an extensive understanding of the opportunities that they could access across the world, together with a grounding in the skills and knowledge needed to access these opportunities, and a deep-rooted belief that they can do anything if only they set their mind to it and work hard enough.

- a school which is extensively linked – in very real and practical ways – with other schools, businesses, a range of organisations and policy-makers, in the local, national and international community, and to which many, many individuals and organisations contribute.

- a school which is able to track its students for the years after they leave the school to see how socially and globally mobile they have become, both in order to learn from them about how to do things better in school, and to intervene to support the students in their life and career choices for years to come.

- a school where striving for social and global mobility is a visible aim that runs through everything that the school does – where it is part of the everyday language of the school, and where all that happens in school is measured against it.

- a school which is seen by everyone in society as a genuine gateway to the future.

This would be a truly Powerful School. And if every school could be like this, just imagine what a transformation there could be in our perception of what schools can do, and in the power of schools themselves to make a huge difference in the world.

What is already being done about social and global mobility? And what can we do better?

The drive to improve social and global mobility is well-recognised as a need in our society – it is part of the social rhetoric of policy makers and social institutions: when people speak of creating 'opportunities' for people, these opportunities often align with greater social mobility, and there is an increasing recognition that this includes global mobility. A look at the landscape not only of schools but of other areas of society such as health and employment shows that there are numerous efforts occurring across a variety of sectors to try to facilitate greater mobility in society: the efforts already mentioned to close the attainment gap in national school examinations, for instance, or to improve the health of people in the lowest socio-economic levels of society, or to create jobs in areas of low unemployment. These efforts are not restricted to areas of social deprivation: society-wide, there is an increasing focus on the whole person and the importance of fulfilment and purpose, as a route to balance and happiness. Choice and opportunity (and purpose) – which are all embedded in social and global mobility – have long been identified as significant factors in contributing to this balance, and they form a major part of the preventative focus that recognises the cost to society of not investing in these elements.

We still find ourselves, however, in a situation where some people have many more opportunities for social and global mobility than others. We know that we cannot change the past, and it is only the future we can affect through our actions now; there is no point bemoaning the past – besides, there is much that is amazing about what has been achieved for humanity in the past years, decades and centuries. None of what is suggested in this book is intended to deflect from all these achievements;

it is designed simply to help us plot a way forward, and to do so by focusing on what schools can achieve by promoting social and global mobility.

Before we begin in detail, it is worth making a few comments. Based on experience and observations, these comments underpin many of the strategies outlined later in this book:

- <u>We need to focus much, much more on global mobility as a means to social mobility.</u> If our young people are to become truly socially mobile, they need to be able to live and work fluently in a world which extends far beyond the geographical limitations of their home towns, and we absolutely need to help them achieve this. Focusing on global mobility as a component of social mobility has an added advantage, however, which benefits the cause of greater social mobility: it can be easier to take a relatively less well-developed concept than social mobility and seek to promote and develop it – there is much less critical baggage or a history of success or failure with which to contend. A disadvantage is that more people need to be convinced of its worth and of how it can work in practice, but this is more than outweighed by the lack of preconceptions in the various stakeholder audiences which the school will wish to engage, and their consequent greater openness to understanding the ideas as the school presents them. This perspective largely explains the inclusion of global mobility alongside social mobility at every point in this book.

- <u>Programmes designed to develop social mobility need to be aimed at all young people, not the few.</u> Programmes which are targeted at specific disadvantaged groups of people rather than at all young people can be very effective, but they can also be limiting in scope and ultimately counter-productive. These programmes can of course work – it stands to reason, in fact, that intensive intervention that responds to the particular needs of the target and is sensitive to their development is going to have a much higher chance of success than general, less well-targeted programmes. However, while such programmes have a short term gain, they have a double downside: they can actually enhance division because they identify groups as being different, and because they do not teach other groups (those less in need of intervention) about the value of the area in question, less ultimately happens in society to promote it. This was the (strong) argument behind greater inclusiveness in schools, so that all children could grow up alongside (and learn about) the value of each child, despite his or her differences and apparent disadvantages. If we target social and global mobility awareness and action at only the least social mobile, we are in effect embedding discrimination and our efforts will ultimately be less effective. We need to overcome our fears that by teaching everyone, we will give some children greater advantages than others: we must adapt our programmes to the needs of individuals, of course, so that they are meaningful and spur these individuals into action, but we also need to be strongly inclusive in our approach.

- It is up to school leaders to make this happen. Any move to develop the social and global mobility of people needs school leaders to take charge of this to make it happen with the very people who it will affect most, and with whom they have regular, everyday contact. Despite the appointed role of policy-makers and education departments in society, and their capacity to govern, regulate and oversee, no-one is as important in the lives of young people as those who exert a personal influence on their daily activity and development – their families, peers and teachers. Nowhere in society, either, are all young people gathered together in a structured and regular way as in schools. This is precisely why action for change needs to start in schools, and why schools need to be the drivers for change. In doing this, school leaders will also be re-orientating schools so that they sit at the centre – at the hub – of change and are able to influence the other elements in society who are concerned with the education of our young people. In practice, this is everyone.

What does a Powerful School look like?

All schools will, quite correctly, place the development of the young person at their heart, and their influence and action can be seen as extending outwards from this point. The spheres of activity in which schools operate, and which they can influence, can therefore broadly be drawn as follows:

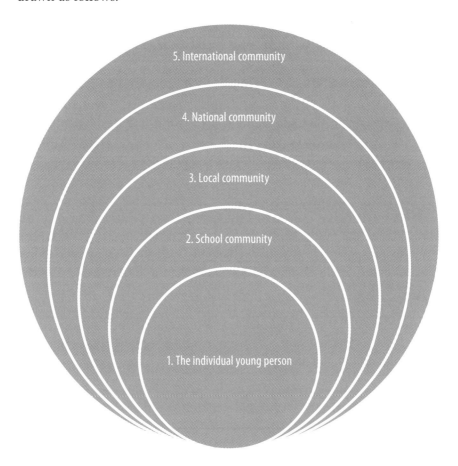

A Powerful School is an enabling school, and it will have an enabling impact on each of these five spheres of activity. It will:

1. enable young people to understand why social and global mobility

are important, and enable them, in practical terms, to become socially and globally mobile;

2. enable the school community to understand, articulate and spread further the school's vision of the importance of social and global mobility, and to contribute practically to the programmes that the school is running;

3. enable the local community to become aware of, and to understand, the drive towards increasing social and global mobility, and to become involved practically in the programmes the school is running, as well as creating further opportunities for practical input;

4. enable national organisations, including businesses and government, to understand and to contribute to developing the social and global mobility of young people (and by extension all people), and to encourage them to direct practical resources towards this aim;

5. enable international schools, organisations, businesses and governmental agencies to understand, adopt and propagate the values and practices which develop social and global mobility, and to engage in practical action that will facilitate the social and global mobility of the students in this school, as well as in many others.

This vision of a Powerful School highlights that there are two main focuses for activity on the part of the school, in each sphere of its activity:

Awareness: developing awareness and understanding of the importance of social and global mobility.

Action: creating practical opportunities to enable young people to become more socially and globally mobile.

Inevitably these focuses overlap – to give an example, the act of developing awareness in young people is in itself a practical step in helping them to become more confident and more knowledgeable, and this self-confidence and understanding are major stepping stones towards greater social and global mobility. The further the school's influence extends from the core of its everyday activity – *ie* the further out into its spheres of activity – the more important the development of awareness and understanding becomes as a precursor to the creation of practical opportunities. Awareness and action are intertwined, and an effective approach will involve both.

It is impossible to be prescriptive about the steps that schools must take to fulfil this vision of a Powerful School. There is no exact 'one-size-fits-all' approach that schools can take to make any of this happen, and schools which engage with the Powerful Schools Vision will themselves generate innovative, forward-thinking, context-specific responses. It is, though, possible to give a flavour of what a Powerful School might look like in this framework, and to prompt ideas about what the school could be doing at each level in order to facilitate social and global mobility.

What could a Powerful School do?

A Powerful School will have a clear, strong vision for social and global mobility, and this vision will be evident both inside the school – explicitly, on the walls and screens, and in the attitudes of students and teachers – and outside the school – visibly on the walls of the school and in the school's digital outreach. A Powerful School will have a reputation for action, for creating opportunities for all its students, and for making a positive difference for young people. It will almost certainly be seen as innovative (until, in due course, the means of developing social and global mobility become universally embedded in schools worldwide), and it will be respected for what it is seeking to do, and for what it is achieving. Crucially, a Powerful School will make visible what it does. By doing so, not only will it be establishing itself as a central hub for the development of social and global mobility, but it will also ensure that it is open to engagement by other people and organisations – other stakeholders, in fact, in the development of young people for a better future.

What, then, could the Powerful School look like in practice? What follows is a picture of what such schools could be if they were truly enabling social and global mobility:

The individual young person (Sphere 1)

The development of the individual young person is obviously the prime focus of schools, and schools are already generally very good already at working at this level to increase social mobility, and – though sometimes less often – global mobility.

Awareness

- The vision will be clear to young people: the curriculum, the co-curricular framework and the language of the school ethos will highlight social and global mobility in the context of personal fulfilment and effective citizenship.
- Students will understand what social and global mobility are, why they are important, and what they can do to develop this in themselves (and others).
- A main thrust of cross-curricular or inter-disciplinary work will be on helping students to understand the world in which they live, and on learning the personal and practical skills that will enable them to live and work confidently and freely within it.

Action

- Students will be well prepared for, and successful in, national and international examinations, and thus able to access opportunities for further study and employment.
- Students will benefit from programmes and opportunities to build their character and develop their self-awareness, self-confidence and self-belief.
- Students will follow programmes that will enable them to develop independence, leadership skills, careers-readiness, teamwork, collaboration, entrepreneurship, digital technology skills, communication skills, and creative and critical thinking skills, and this development will be carefully tracked, monitored and evaluated so that the programmes are always improving, and genuinely work for each individual.

The school community (Sphere 2)

Awareness

- Curricular and interdisciplinary programmes will be in place to give students an understanding of the importance of collaboration, as well as to develop actual collaborative skills, with the opportunities to practise these.

- Teachers and support staff will be trained in an awareness of social and global mobility, and how to develop this awareness and practice in young people.

Action

- Students will have significant and frequent opportunities to work collectively on major projects that have a social impact.
- Teachers will have opportunities to become external advocates of schools as proponents of social and global mobility.
- Programmes will be in place for families and all those connected with schools to understand the value of social and global mobility and how to contribute to practical programmes to support this inside school and in the school's wider networks.
- The wider school community will be actively involved in creating programmes and opportunities which support students and also reach out to the local, national and international communities.

The local community (Sphere 3)

Awareness

- All local people, including but not limited to those already connected in some way to the school, will understand that they have a stake in the school and in its work, and that there are opportunities for everyone to help make a difference for young people through connecting them with the wider world and possibilities for the future.

Action

- Very practical links with local businesses, charities *etc* will exist to enable programmes of work experience for students (schools often have an excellent tradition already of doing this).
- Local people will have multiple and varied opportunities to come into school to mentor and teach young people.
- The school will be a hub for lifelong learning, potentially in partnership with other organisations, including Further Education colleges, to enable members of the community of all ages to earn qualifications that will allow them to develop their interests and work choices.

The national community (Sphere 4)

Awareness

- The school's digital presence will reflect its goals for social and global mobility, and the school will engage actively with the media and social media to propagate awareness of these goals.
- The school will be active in communicating with national government, national businesses and policy-makers about how it is promoting social and global mobility.

Action

- Students will have opportunities to come into contact with people from other parts of the country, both because they are invited into school to, for example, speak, run courses and engage with students, and because students are able to go out of school for day and multi-day visits.
- Policy-makers at national level will regularly be invited into school to see what is going on, and to learn about the concrete possibilities that exist to develop social and global mobility.
- The school will have significant and meaningful partnerships with universities, so that students can begin to make the transition to Higher Education more easily and naturally while still at school, with study courses, on-site visits *etc*, all of which could be developed so that they are available to other members of the school and local community.

The international community (Sphere 5)

Awareness

- A detailed programme will exist, embedded into the school curriculum and available (in different forms) to others connected with the school, that raises cultural awareness of life in different countries around the world, and different socio-economic groups within these countries.
- In addition to the language learning programmes already followed in school, a programme or programmes will be in place to give an overview of world languages, introducing students to the basics in a number of key languages.

- The school will be active in a wide number of networks, sharing information and best practice with schools and organisations around the world, and will have attracted the interest of international organisations and policy-makers.

Action

- An active and sustained programme of links will exist with schools around the world, so that every student in school has thorough and regular opportunities to:
  - become curious and learn about different cultures, and become familiar with them.
  - connect with their peers abroad and spend enough quality time with them, probably virtually (*eg* through Skype/video-conferencing) to be able to build a number of personal relationships.
  - travel abroad and live for increasingly long periods of time overseas, and increasingly independently and meaningfully, which is all possible before the age of 18, *eg*:

- An active programme of links will exist with international organisations who promote social and global mobility, including charities and international businesses, which will both engage the organisations in understanding the power of schools to make change happen, and lead to students developing a global awareness by engaging in:
  - researching and exploring life overseas
  - fundraising for projects overseas
  - international work experience
- Students, teachers and others in and connected with the school will have opportunities for further in-depth and perhaps accelerated or intensive language learning through out-of-

school links with external organisations (*eg* local universities, language schools *etc*).

EXERCISE: What else would you imagine a Powerful School might look like? Take the ideas above, explore them, think about them. What would you add?

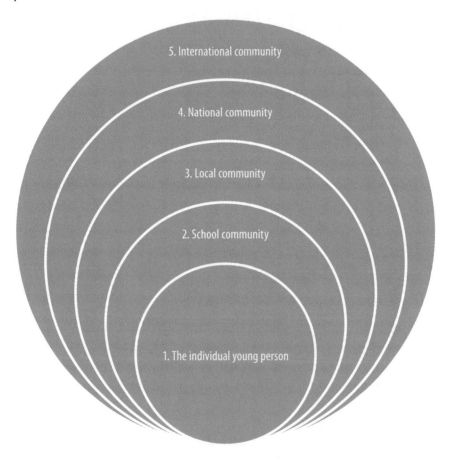

When you describe each of your school's spheres of activity, what would you ideally like to find in each one? What would turn your school into a Powerful School?

Enhancing the power: working with other schools

Working with other schools is key to successful propagation of ideas and action, and to changing mindsets. Being part of a prevailing movement is far more likely to be effective than working alone, and because of this, school leaders should take every opportunity possible to share their ideas about the development of social and global mobility, together with details of programmes they have developed, and ways in which they have engaged organisations and groups at all five levels of activity and influence. Such opportunities can arise:

- informally, in discussion with local school leaders and contacts at schools further afield,
- at local school network events (*eg* cluster groups),
- at education conferences locally, nationally and internationally,
- at any event or group where other schools are present.

In doing this, school leaders will be inspiring other schools and showing them pathways so that they too can identify and spread their influence. It stands to reason that the more schools that are aligned with this vision of Powerful Schools, and the more they too are working on its principles, the more likely it is that change will happen.

EXERCISE: what are your links like with other schools? List all the schools you can think of and consider how strong your connections are. What does this list and the distribution of these schools suggest to you about where you might need to build more relationships?

Schools locally	What kind of connection do you have?	How strong is this connection? 1 (poor)- 5 (excellent)
Schools further afield (national)	What kind of connection do you have?	How strong is this connection? 1 (poor)- 5 (excellent)

Schools abroad (international)	What kind of connection do you have?	How strong is this connection? 1 (poor)- 5 (excellent)

The key to effective action on a large scale is always to engage many, many partners. Collaboration and co-operation in pursuit of a shared vision can make anything possible. And if a school leader is still tempted to wonder why this task has fallen in their lap rather than that of, for example, government, then they should remember that it is schools which ultimately are best placed to be able to affect, directly, the lives of young people and the society in which these young people will grow up. The question is not so much 'why?' as 'why not?' – and 'why not now?'.

Where is your starting point?

As part of the process of working out what the school does well and what it needs to do better, we can translate the levels of a school's influence identified above, and a school's focuses for activity, into a matrix which is a useful starting point for reflection on what the school already does to enable social and global mobility. This is a precursor to the more detailed initial audit outlined in Chapter 4.

	How well does our school do in each of these areas?	
	Awareness: developing awareness of social and global mobility	*Action*: practical skills/development and action to develop social and global mobility
Sphere 1: the individual young person		
Sphere 2: the school community		
Sphere 3: the local community		
Sphere 4: the national community		
Sphere 5: the international community		

EXERCISE: take a moment to think about how you would evaluate your school according to the matrix of questions above. You do not yet have the data you will gather from an audit – that will come later, and you will be able to refine your judgements as you base them on solid data – but what is your impression now? What is your overall sense of how well you are doing, on a scale of 1 (poor) to 5 (excellent)? Write down your scores and keep them – they are your preliminary judgements, and they will help guide some of the decisions you take about how to proceed further.

*****

You are already starting to build up ideas about what schools – your school – could do to improve the social and global mobility of young people and society more broadly. You are already starting to think about what you are doing well and what you could do better. You are already on the journey.

Chapter 3

Who is going to make this happen? Who are your stakeholders?

Schools sit within a vast network of connected people, all of whom have a stake or interest in what happens in schools. If schools understand this, they can begin to engage with these relationships more effectively. This will help focus activity on social and global mobility, with schools at the centre of this activity. There are numerous stakeholders in schools, and this means that there are numerous groups of people which schools can engage in order to translate their latent power into powerful action to facilitate social and global mobility. Ideas for engaging each of these groups of stakeholders are examined in turn and in detail in Chapter 7, and you can skip ahead to this section if you are seeking immediate inspiration. The purpose of this short chapter is to introduce schools to the range of people and organisations who can help schools pursue their vision, and with whom schools can engage more effectively. It will start to prompt creative thinking about who can help you.

The following broad types of stakeholders will be familiar to schools:

- Students

- Teachers
- Non-teaching staff
- Volunteers in school
- School boards
- Parents/carers
- Grandparents/wider families
- Former students
- Community groups – charities, voluntary groups
- Businesses – small, medium, large
- Universities and further education institutions
- Government – local, national
- National organisations – charities, support groups, political groups, lobbying groups
- People of influence – local, national, international
- International relationships – organisations, businesses, movements
- Other schools and school-to-school networks

Each of these groups of stakeholders has their own particular motivations and their own particular potential contribution – *ie* they will have their own reasons to be engaged with the vision, and they will have different resources to do so. These are explored in more detail in Chapter 5. Many of these will overlap, and – as regards motivations in particular – it is possible only to talk in the broadest of terms, as people are all individuals and have their own priorities and vastly differing capacities to be able to contribute to a vision of Powerful Schools. To give an example of this potential overlap and differing priorities, a school may perhaps count amongst its parent body some parents whose role is entirely focused on managing immediate family needs (food, work, children) and other parents who might perhaps have privileged access to governmental, media or business sources which could be of use to the school in facilitating connections and communication with other stakeholders.

A reminder about power and its use: schools are generally very good at treating children fairly, as individuals, regardless of family background;

this all comes down to respect for the individual and his/her particular strengths and circumstances. If schools apply the same principles in reaching out to all their stakeholders, then they will be able to manage the process of extending their power in an ethical and properly grounded way. They do need to reach out, however, and overcome their fear of power – if they don't, then they risk missing the opportunity to make a difference.

Who are your stakeholders?

The first step in this process is to understand who the stakeholders in schools actually are. To be able to conceptualise, and then to approach, stakeholders in a systematic and comprehensive (and manageable) way, schools are almost certainly going to need to group their stakeholders into categories. It can be helpful to do this firstly by listing them under the headings of the five spheres of Powerful Schools identified in the picture of a school in Chapter 2. This grouping of stakeholders will vary from school to school depending on existing relationships: for example, a school which has a well-developed relationship – perhaps through teacher-training – with a university in the same city, may classify that university under 'local community', although other universities will still belong under the 'national community' heading. Universities overseas, meanwhile, will probably sit under the 'international community' heading, unless the school has particularly close links with them – enough to count them as, say, an extension of the school community.

In broad terms, then, and bearing in mind, of course, the caveat above about how motivations and groups overlap, the stakeholders in schools are likely to divide roughly as follows:

SPHERE 1: The individual young person	Students
SPHERE 2: The school community	Teachers Non-teaching staff School boards Volunteers in school Parents/immediate carers

SPHERE 3:	Wider families, including grandparents
The local community	Former students
	Community groups, including charities and voluntary groups
	Local businesses – small, medium and large
	Other adults
	Local government and local education departments
	Further education institutions
	Other schools
SPHERE 4:	National Government
The national community	National businesses
	People of national influence
	National organisations – charities/support groups/political groups/lobbying groups
	Universities
	Other schools
SPHERE 5:	People of international influence – local, national, international
The international community	International relationships – organisations, businesses, movements
	International governmental organisations
	Other schools

One of the first exercises that schools will need to do is to work out where their own stakeholders fit into this matrix:

EXERCISE: Think carefully about your school and all your stakeholders. How close to them do you feel you are? Where would you place them in the following table? Be specific and divide groups into appropriate sub-groups depending on your specific context.

SPHERE 1: The individual young person	
SPHERE 2: The school community	
SPHERE 3: The local community	
SPHERE 4: The national community	
SPHERE 5: The international community	

This exercise will provide you with a working understanding of who your stakeholders are. Chapter 5 will take this further, exploring the motivations of the stakeholder groups, and their potential to contribute to the Powerful Schools Vision. It will look in more detail at how schools can engage these groups, using the power of the different approaches embedded in each sphere of a school's activity. First, however, the next chapter – Chapter 4 – explores how schools can plan for change.

Chapter 4

Planning for change

Really good planning is organic: it is underpinned by a strong and clear vision, but it adapts and changes as more information and evidence comes to light. This is especially the case when the vision behind the planning will take the organisation forward into new territory, exploring new ideas and ways of working in order to make a difference. To put it simply, ideas and thinking that have yet to be invented cannot be incorporated into a first draft of a strategic plan, but will need to be identified and absorbed into it as the plan evolves.

When the scope of the vision extends beyond the immediate range of influence of an organisation – as the Powerful Schools Vision does – then it is almost inevitable that this will demand not only new thinking, but new forms of action, and as these emerge and become clearer, these processes too will need to be incorporated into an evolving plan. Strategic planning for visionary change is by necessity fluid, and school leaders should not be afraid of embracing this fluidity. Put simply, your first strategic plan will most likely evolve radically as you embark on the process of strategic change.

Great plans, however, do depend on accurate knowledge and understanding; the more you know about what you are doing, the more effective the plan is likely to be. Moreover, for a plan to be effective, it has to be owned and managed by people who are committed to it, and the more people who understand what the vision is about, and who buy into it, the greater the likelihood that the plan will gain traction. Successful plans also need skilled planners – people who can translate evidence and ideas into concrete and achievable action points. In short, great strategic plans have three key main elements:

- Exploring / reflecting / thinking
- Communicating
- Target-setting

In preparing for change, these three elements need to operate together, in combinations which will vary depending on the specific circumstances of the school and its relationships with stakeholders. It is not a linear process, whereby exploring and understanding what is needed is followed by communication of these ideas, which leads in turn to the establishment of a plan, which is then merely implemented. Exploring and communicating are in any case closely linked: without clear lines of two-way communication, it is harder to develop an accurate understanding of what is actually happening. Sometimes, explicitly communicating the vision first will be necessary in order to engage people sufficiently so that you can explore with them what is currently happening, and what could happen. Sometimes the planning will come first – whoever is leading this process may need to sit down, plan a course of action based on current information, and work with this, gathering more information en route and modifying the plan accordingly.

The Powerful Schools Vision is one whose pathways to success have yet to be constructed, let alone trodden, and the process of moving towards the vision demands constant interrogation of the plan which is put together to facilitate action. It requires nimbleness of thought, and the capacity to think, connect with others, and work in ways which have yet to be invented. Key to its success will be constant evaluation, and adaptation, and this is where senior leaders need to embrace – and be invigorated by – the fluidity of the process.

Exploring: the auditing process

Of course, the more we can understand the current state of affairs, the more informed we can be, and the better the judgements we make.

Any practical strategies aimed at developing and focusing the power of schools to make a difference to social and global mobility will benefit by starting with a detailed audit of how these groups currently contribute to this goal.

Audits usually have a dual purpose – firstly, they identify information and develop understanding, and secondly, the process of conducting the audit is an opportunity to engage stakeholders further in the area under scrutiny. The purpose of an audit process focused on social and global mobility is to ascertain, as best possible, what is known in school about the groups identified as stakeholders, what they understand about social and global mobility, and what they currently contribute to a drive towards this mobility, as well as to the power of the school to make a difference.

The auditing process is likely to have 4 stages, some of which may run concurrently, and which will certainly be repeated in cycles, as more information emerges and more ideas are generated and implemented or tested in action:

1. information-gathering about what others are doing to engage with social and global mobility;

2. internal audit, based on the experience of those running the audit;

3. stakeholder audit; and

4. regular evaluative audit.

Auditing is all about finding out what is happening now, but audits with the purpose of prompting change can (and almost certainly should) also start the process of suggesting answers. It is important that those gathering information or conducting the audit keep an open mind and do not limit themselves by, for example, measuring what they find out only against their prior experience of what works successfully in school. A significant part of the future strategic work of the school, its stakeholders and partners will be to make things happen in ways that they have not happened before. The school can do this by imagining and creating ideas, finding innovative ways to implement these, and, along the way, developing best practice to share with others. Everyone engaged in the process of exploring needs to sign up to the discipline of keeping an open mind, a powerful imagination and a positive, strong, 'can-do' focus on the vision, which may lead to unexpected and new, invented outcomes.

Looking at each of the stages of the auditing process in turn, it is nonetheless possible to identify some very practical strategies to start the process by helping to frame activity that is likely to lead towards a successful outcome.

1. Information-gathering

General information-gathering is important to set the scene for those conducting the audit, and to prepare them for the range of possibilities that they may encounter. If integrated into the overall strategic development process aimed at creating a Powerful School in practice, it will also continue to feed and stimulate thinking about the why, what and how of schools as proponents of social and global mobility. The more examples and ideas that can be found to support the Powerful Schools Vision, the easier schools will find it to articulate and communicate this vision, and to influence others to engage with it. This book is an initial source of ideas and thoughts in this respect, but a host of other sources are waiting to be explored, including:

- inter-school networks – what are other schools doing to develop social and global mobility?
- local, national and international organisations focusing on social and global mobility – what have they found that works?
- research and thinking – why are social and global mobility philosophically and historically important? Why are they relevant in the 21st century?
- perspectives from others – anyone connected with or interested in schools, young or old: what do they think about social and global mobility? What do they see as possible? What have they heard of or encountered in practice?

Different schools will have different means of gathering information; whichever way they choose, however, needs to pass the acid tests of:

- authority – will people trust and listen to what is reported back?
- sustainability – can this approach to information-gathering be sustained in the long run, irrespective of changes in personnel, and mindful of other pressures and roles that people have to play in school? Will the project be carried through?

An obvious way to make information-gathering a central part of the development of a vision is to set up a working group, led by a member of the senior leadership team, but the effectiveness of this approach will depend on the quality and quantity of time allocated for the task, and the commitment and skill of the people involved. There is a strong case to be made for engaging in some communication more broadly within the school community (and possibly the wider community) before setting up such a group, so that the load is spread widely amongst equally passionate members, although school leaders will recognise that large working groups are not always very effective. Drive and clarity of vision – and a commitment to the cause – are everything: they are what will keep the group forging ahead when more immediate school-based issues require attention and/or demand precedence.

2. Internal audit

This is a crucial step, and is treated in detail below, with matrices which can be used subsequently for stakeholders and for ongoing evaluation. The purpose of this audit is for the senior leadership team - who need to be at the heart of developing the Powerful Schools Vision, and who will need to be driving it - to take as close a look as possible at how social and global mobility are currently treated in the school and in the school's relationships with its stakeholder groups. This process of auditing has a number of functions in addition to helping the leadership team understand what the school currently does to further social and global mobility:

- it helps the leadership team refine their understanding of who their stakeholders are;
- by highlighting what the leadership team doesn't know as well as what it does know, it provides the leadership team with a clearer set of questions for the next stage, *ie* the stakeholder audits;

- the process itself is empowering: it helps members of the leadership team to clarify, explore and extend their thinking about the potential power of schools as hubs of social and global mobility;
- it will inevitably stimulate ideas about what the school could do in the future, all of which need to be retained, recorded, and woven into an ongoing strategy.

3. Stakeholder audit

On the back of the results of the internal audit, it is tempting to rush into stakeholder audits, in order to find out what the stakeholder groups think they are doing to contribute to the aim of social and global mobility, but the danger here is that by rushing, you will gather together a far narrower and less diverse group of enthusiasts than you could if you waited until you engaged more people. It stands to reason that the larger the available stakeholder group from which you can draw when you seek to involve stakeholders proactively, the more representative and diverse this group is likely to be, which in turn means that they are more likely to be more accurate in their assessment of their current activity. If you can wait until you have developed clearer messages and the means to communicate effectively with your stakeholders, then you will be able to draw on a wider field of people with greater potential, for more extensive creative thinking, and almost certainly have larger spheres of potential influence.

It makes sense, therefore, to interweave communication and engagement strategies, explored in detail in Chapter 7, with an exploration and audit strategy, depending on the grasp you feel you have on the stakeholder groups. A school with close relationships with local business groups, or with local or national government, will likely decide to engage these groups in an audit at an earlier stage than schools which have yet to build these networks through their communication. A rule of thumb is to work first with the groups to whom you have most access in their entirety – all students, for example, and teachers and parents – before moving out into other fields.

4. Regular evaluative audit

Evaluation is essential in order to feed back into the process at regular intervals, certainly of no less than a year, and potentially every six months. Regular evaluative audits, or reviews, enable the leadership team to ensure that they are keeping on track with their action. By drawing on the insights of the stakeholders as well as their own perceptions, they will be able to see how effective they are being. Regular evaluation of action keeps people focused, and ensures that the strategic plan is 'alive' and continuously adapted to drive forward action.

The internal audit

Choosing the team

The choice of person (or group) to lead this audit is really important. People who run schools know that if you want something done, you need to ask someone who is passionate about it to do it, and this is a good reason to ensure that whoever conducts this audit is/are absolutely committed to extending the power of schools to influence social and global mobility. School leaders also know that creating committees or working groups to solve a problem or facilitate strategic development can draw a number of people into a task, which spreads the load but can also slow down the accomplishment of that task, simply because time is such an issue, and with the demands on people's time (and the constraints of timetables *etc*), it can be hard to get key staff together at a time and in a place where they have the brain space to consider and act on new thinking. In the end, the choice of person or people to run the audit will have to be school-specific, but there are various guiding principles which will help ensure that the project is a success:

- Consider appointing someone formally to this role, and recognising this financially and/or with time. This will depend to an enormous extent on how much flexibility your school has with its budget; many schools will have little or no flexibility, and will have to be inventive about how they can build the engagement of the community with minimal leadership. Remember, though, the importance of social and global mobility and the need for schools to do something to drive this process – in short, we cannot afford for this not to happen, and conceivably the role is as important as that of, for example, a literacy co-ordinator, even if it has less immediate – and less easily trackable – effects for the young people in the school. If this drive is successful, however, and schools are transformed into central and influential hubs in respect of social and global mobility, then the students in the school today and in the future will be directly and indirectly positively impacted throughout their lives by the change that schools are making happen. Leading this drive is an important role.

- Only select people who are truly committed to making action happen, and who are passionate about the issues highlighted in Chapter 1 of this book. If the preliminary audit is to be conducted before all staff are introduced to the concepts and the potential of a drive towards social and global mobility, then ensure that the person or people chosen to conduct the audit is/ are fully immersed in the issues, and feel personally driven to want to make change happen. Forging a path into new territory is not always easy; forging a path when the task is seen as an unwelcome burden is even harder. Passion and drive see people over many a hurdle; make sure that the people at the heart of this drive have this in abundance.

- Only select effective people – people who will get things done, and who are solutions-focused. The more creative the thinker, the better, but the audit itself will also need a clear head for data and the ability to choose the most appropriate means to gather this data.

- Ensure that whoever conducts the audit is aware of, and has access to, every area of school life. Often, there are only a few people in school who have a complete understanding of everything that goes on in school. This suggests either that a senior leader needs to take on this role, or else that a group of individuals needs to take it on, so that all areas of school can be covered effectively.

- There is always the option of an external auditor, *ie* bringing in an individual or group of people to look at what the school is doing. The major advantage is that of time – *ie* by employing someone who can devote time to the project which will not detract from everyday school activity – and perhaps also of bringing specific additional skills into school. Schools audit and evaluate all the time, but not as much or in as focused a way as people and groups in, for example, corporate bodies who make it their daily focus, and schools can certainly learn from experience generated in other sectors. The major disadvantages with this approach are the potential (high) cost, the potential lack of deep understanding of a school that an outsider usually has, the fact that the individual/group chosen may not fully understand the school's nascent vision about social and global mobility, and the loss of an opportunity to use the auditing process to engage immediate stakeholders in school. On balance, schools are likely to veer away from this route – but it may just be that there is someone within the school's stakeholder groups who is predisposed to help, who has time and relevant expertise and who understands the school thoroughly.

- Ensure that from the outset, any individual, group or committee establishes a clear working brief, allocates roles, creates an action plan with a timeline, and sticks to it. If it is not a senior leader who is running this process, then make sure that there is close senior leadership oversight of what is happening, largely so that the senior leadership never lose sight of the progress that is being made in this area. Ultimately, social and global mobility are so fundamental to a school's purpose that they have to sit at the heart of the school's vision and daily activity – senior leaders have to own them and live them.

Planning for the internal audit: working out when to do what, and how
Planning when to do anything in school has to take into account multiple variables, and there is never usually an absolutely right time to start any development processes. Each school will have its own specific circumstances that influence when and how it chooses to start the foundation work that will lead to a strategy to develop greater social and global mobility for its current students and further afield. A number of principles may be helpful, however, for school leaders planning the development process:

- *Transparency*

As noted above, there are often only a few people who actually know everything that is going on in school and who have an overview of school strategy. This happens through necessity – people are usually fully immersed in their own specific areas of activity (which usually coincide with their particular interests and passions). In a process which seeks to reconceptualise schools as hubs of powerful activity, however, the more that everyone in schools knows about what goes on in their school, the better. Transparency brings understanding, and understanding what the process of developing a vision for social and global mobility is all about is a fundamental building block of engagement. Embedding this as a principle from the outset will help engage a wider field of stakeholders, and will also – a very useful offshoot – help school leaders to clarify and refine their message, so as to ensure that it is communicated clearly: one of the key testing grounds for how new ideas and strategies are formulated is when they are brought out into the open and subjected to critical scrutiny. When school leaders start explaining what they are doing, and why, it is an opportunity to see if their audiences grasp this and are equally excited by it; if not, the message needs to be refined and targeted more carefully.

- *Communication*

Transparency is integrally linked with communication. As for most large organisations, effective communication is a real challenge for schools, and it is worth looking more generally at communication as part of the engagement process – *ie* how schools can communicate more effectively with, and engage more effectively with, all stakeholders about what does, can and could happen in school. Traditional communication methods of parent meetings and letters home struggle to communicate the voice of the school in a world where people are busy, preoccupied with many concerns, and also bombarded by endless information from numerous sources. Schools need to think carefully about how to win the fight to be heard above the other noise of society. Part of this will come down to means of communication – how can schools tap into other streams of information that their stakeholders will access, including digital communication and other media, and – crucially – word-of-mouth? Part of the answer will also lie in frequency of communication, and a strong focus on getting the school's message out clearly and often.

- *Openness to ideas and nimbleness of thought*

  This is really important. As noted earlier, forging into new territory does not come with a road map, and schools will need to subscribe to a discipline of open-mindedness if they are to create the way forward. They need not to see this as a linear process – ideas for future action will be prompted by the information that emerges from questions around what is already being done, and this cannot necessarily be predicted. This is a crucially important point – the process of moving towards a strong, implemented vision of social and global mobility in schools requires a discipline of thought around a belief in change and a belief that anything is possible if you set your mind to it.

How to conduct the internal audit

How schools choose to conduct audits is entirely up them – school leaders just need to make sure that however they do it, the process is going to result in a reliable overview of the current state of play, as this is going to be the basis for informed decisions about strategy and action. Elements to consider include:

- *Timeliness* – make sure that the process is a nimble one, and is not going to take too long, because otherwise the information gained may soon be out of date, and/or there will not be enough time left in the planning cycle to prepare for change for the next school year. A good rule of thumb is to limit the information-gathering to the first term or semester of a school year (maximum), so that there is time to reflect on the outcomes and consider how to start introducing or piloting new strategies for the new school year.

- *Comprehensiveness* – every area of school life needs to be looked at. This will include every curriculum area, every programme concerned with student development, every co-curricular area (every club and out-of-school activity) and every external relationship and opportunity for students, teachers and other members of the school community.

What to ask and how to record it

The key question in this audit, on which a judgement needs to be taken, is:

In each of the five spheres of the school's activity, how well does our school

(a) develop awareness of social and global mobility; and

(b) engage in practical skills development and/or action to develop social and global mobility?

In the initial audit, the goal is to understand what is actually going on in school and in the wider school community to help develop social and global mobility, and to come up with a broad judgement which will be a baseline against which future progress can be measured. This two-part question can be mapped on to the five spheres of a school's activity, resulting in a matrix of ten areas, each of which requires a judgement:

	How well does our school do in each of these areas?	
	Awareness: developing awareness of social and global mobility	*Action*: practical skills development and/or action to develop social and global mobility
Sphere 1: the individual young person		
Sphere 2: the school community		
Sphere 3: the local community		
Sphere 4: the national community		
Sphere 5: the international community		

If you already use a tried and tested system of recording judgements in school for other aspects of tracking progress and development, then the simplest approach is to transfer this existing system across and use it for the process of auditing social and global mobility too. If such a system is not in place, consider using one of the following ways to record your judgements in the table above:

- using a 'traffic lights' system, *ie*
  - green – yes, we do this really well indeed

- amber – we do this, but there is room for improvement and to do more
- red – we don't really do this at all
- using a 1-5 system
  - 5 – we do this extremely well
  - 4 – we do this quite well
  - 3 – we do this, but there is room for improvement
  - 2 – we do a bit of this, but not really very much
  - 1 – we don't really do this at all

This is the goal of an audit – a simple, clear, immediately understandable judgement on how well the school is developing social and global mobility. In order to make the judgement, however, schools need evidence about what they are actually doing. It is possible for anyone in school to fill in this matrix straight away with their impressions of how things are going – in fact, this was the purpose of the exercise at the end of Chapter 2 – but in order to make the judgement as reliable as possible, the evidence gathered to support any conclusion ideally needs to be as comprehensive and detailed as possible, and this is why a structured audit is such a good idea.

How to get the information you need

The basic question is a straightforward one: what is happening in school? The challenge in answering this question lies primarily in understanding (and helping the people conducting the audit to understand) what each of the two main focuses (awareness-raising and practical skills development) might look like in practice. What are the auditors actually looking for? If they are going to ask teachers in charge of specific areas to report on what they do to support social and global mobility, how are they going to make sure that the teachers are given a steer on what sort of areas they are looking for?

Part of the answer to this lies in engaging, and communicating effectively with, everyone who is going to be involved in gathering information, and this is treated in detail in Chapter 7, which takes each of the stakeholder groups in turn and explores ideas about how to involve them in the work of the school. At this early stage, not only do the auditors themselves have to have a grounded understanding of what they are looking for, while keeping an open mind about what they will find, but they also need to make sure that anyone who is going to be responsible for answering the questions they ask also develops this grounded understanding. This means that the auditor or auditing team needs to frame the context of the questions so that they give an understanding of what social and global mobility are, why they are important, and (very broadly) what programmes or activity to support their development might look like in practice, so that people have a clearer idea of what they need to report on.

What can sometimes help in this respect is to ask the questions as specifically as possible, *eg:*

- what is happening in English lessons in Year 7 (or 8/9/10 *etc*) to develop awareness of social and global mobility?
- what are the personal development programmes in Year 2 (or 3/4/5 *etc*) contributing to students' awareness of social and global mobility?
- what practical action is happening in the Year 11 careers programme to develop social and global mobility?

However, it can very easily become time-consuming to construct subject-specific questionnaires, which will most likely limit the progress that a team working on this area will make, and it can also have the effect of limiting the scope for departments to collaborate and to help one another understand how the basic questions can be interpreted in practice. A far more sensible solution all round is just to keep the questions simple.

It is especially important for an initial audit not to have a checklist of points of action against which departments or areas of school life can measure themselves. An initial audit is the first step on a journey of exploration about which actions in school can contribute to social and global mobility, and part of its purpose is to get people thinking about what they do, and (by extension) what they might do better. The questions asked need therefore to be open, not closed (ie not 'are you doing X?' but 'what are you doing?'), and they also need to be simple and understandable:

- what, if anything, are you/your department doing to develop awareness of social and global mobility?
- what, if anything, are you/your department doing to develop practical skills and/or action that will lead to greater social and global mobility?

Another possibility is to ask slightly more refined questions, if this helps to facilitate understanding:

- what, if anything, are you/your department doing to contribute to developing awareness of social and global mobility?
- what, if anything, are you/your department doing to contribute to developing practical skills and/or action that will lead to greater social and global mobility?

The choice of language and the nuances of engaging with the staff of a school are entirely at the discretion of the school itself. It is, though, the 'what' that you want to find out first. It is a less loaded and less complex question than 'how', which assumes that something is actually happening, and requires people to wrestle with broader questions of how they are contributing more generally to the skills of individual students to, for example, think critically or believe in their abilities. The question of 'how are you doing this?' is perhaps best left for a follow-up audit, when it comes to identifying and sharing best practice, but auditors/ auditing teams will be able to make their own judgement on this too. Equally, they can also make a judgement on the extent to which they want to use the opportunity presented by an initial audit to solicit ideas and thoughts about what they or the school might do in the future:

- what do you think you could perhaps do in the future to develop awareness of social and global mobility?
- what do you think you could perhaps do in the future to develop practical skills that will lead to greater social and global mobility?
- what do you think other areas of the school could perhaps do in the future to develop awareness of social and global mobility?
- what do you think other areas of the school could perhaps do in the future to develop practical skills that will lead to greater social and global mobility?

Remember that you want to find out how subject/department/faculty/ groups of staff and students *etc* are engaged with all five spheres of school activity, not just with the individual student, although this will almost certainly be the area where the most activity currently takes place. This leads on to the second main challenge in getting the information the auditing team needs: how can the team target the questions systematically at each area of school life, while not making these questions repetitive or onerous?

Sound advice is to be as focused as possible in targeting the questions at specific areas of school, sub-dividing these as many times as necessary to get to a stage where it will be easy for someone reading the question to understand exactly what is being asked of them and of the area(s) of school of which they have most knowledge and awareness. It is probably worth isolating whole-school areas like academic attainment and external examination scores and treating them separately, because this information will be gathered centrally anyway, and taking academic scores out of the equation will enable the staff in charge of curriculum and other areas to focus on what else they do that really contributes either to raising awareness of social and global mobility in one of the five spheres of the school's activity, or to developing skills or putting in place practical action that will support social and global mobility.

Who to ask in the initial audit
This is again entirely up to the school, although a good starting point would be:

- staff in charge of academic faculties / school departments;
- staff in charge of pastoral areas (*eg* Heads of Year);
- staff with responsibility for any area in school (*eg* student behaviour, careers);
- all individual staff – teaching and non-teaching.

There are many very good reasons for asking for student input at this stage too, and this is entirely up to the judgement of the senior leadership team. The more people who are asked, the more thorough the initial self-evaluation will be, but the more-consuming and resource-intensive the process. Moreover, the further out the school reaches into the groups of stakeholders, to ask what they think, the more effort needs to be placed on developing strong engagement strategies, allied with clear and focused communication strategies, so that these groups (many of whom may have only a tenuous relationship with the school) have a clear and balanced understanding of what the school is doing, and why, and how this fits into the school's overall purpose and activity.

Schools can choose who they ask in this initial audit – it is entirely up to them. They must just be aware, in making a judgement based on the data they collect, of what impact their choice of groups will have on the scope of the audit, and they must be mindful of this in drawing overarching conclusions. Most initial audits are incomplete in their coverage – this is fine, as they will still gather very useful data, but schools just need to remember that there will be other sources of information and insight which they will want to access in the future.

If the school decides that the principal focus of this initial audit is to be on people who work in school regularly, and who have responsibility for running and developing programmes of study, and/or people in direct contact with students, then a number of different methods exist to gather the insights that these staff hold. These include:

- a written or online questionnaire aimed at teachers with responsibility for all the key areas in school identified by the leadership and auditing team;
- structured individual interviews with key people;
- mixed 'focus groups' drawn from a cross-section of the school staff or even school community;
- oral or written feedback from a whole-staff session where all staff contribute in groups to answering the questions.

There are numerous ways in which such activities can be structured and facilitated, but whichever route the school takes, or whichever combination of routes, the important elements are the clarity of the questions and the comprehensive coverage of the school's activity, so that as much information as possible can inform the next steps. Whatever approach you decide to adopt, keep the questions as simple as possible so that the impact of the questionnaire on staff workload is as light as possible. Keep returning to the key questions that you want to have answered: *In each of the five spheres of the school's activity, how well does our school (a) develop awareness of social and global mobility; and (b) engage in practical skills development and/or action to develop social and global mobility?*

How to manage the data gathered

There is potentially a very large amount of data that can be gathered during this initial audit. The more data that can be gathered, the more grounded the judgement that can be made on how well the school is doing in each of its spheres of activity, but this does present a problem of how to store and how to interpret this data. Recording and analysing the data needs very careful thought. The raw data that will come from gathering information about exactly what the school is doing will be the basis of the judgements, but if it is used to make judgements without being situated in an overall balanced picture of what <u>isn't</u> happening, as well as what <u>is</u>, then it risks distorting the judgement (and turning it into a series of anecdotes). Raw data needs to be kept because it is the basis of the judgements made, and so needs to be available for external interrogation. However, it also needs to be summarised, in order to provide a basis for the judgement score. This can be recorded in a similar format to the overall judgement table, but tells a story that explains the score (or traffic light colour) that will be transferred to the overall judgement table, *eg*:

Sphere 1: the individual young person

Awareness: developing awareness of social and global mobility

EXAMPLE: Some very good awareness-raising of social mobility occurs in the Personal and Social Development programme in Years 8 and 9. However, there is no cohesive strand which runs through the school curriculum to highlight social mobility as a specific goal, and there has been little or no focus on global mobility as a concept in the school curriculum, although students are taught about international affairs in approximately 60% of curriculum areas. (Amber/3)

Sphere 1: the individual young person

Action: practical skills development or action to develop social and global mobility

EXAMPLE: The careers programme in Years 9-12 provides excellent opportunities for work experience and also placement into Higher Education. 95% of students go on to a positive work or study destination on leaving school. Examination scores are well above the national average, and this aids social mobility. However, there is little or no evidence to suggest that students feel confident in their ability to be able to move freely, eg to live and work abroad, or to work with different cultures. (Amber/3)

Sphere 2: the school community

Awareness: developing awareness of social and global mobility

EXAMPLE: Some teachers are passionate about social mobility and a (smaller) number are committed to developing global mobility in their students, although they are not always clear about how this might fit into a whole school strategy. Non-teaching staff do not feel that they have a role in school strategy. Other members of the school community were not asked for the purposes of this initial audit. (Amber/2)

When all the information from an initial audit is gathered together, it will provide extremely valuable insights into:

- what social and global mobility mean in practice;
- what the school does well, and what it doesn't, to promote and develop social and global mobility;
- who in the school knows, understands, and believes what about social and global mobility;
- how the school already engages with other elements of society, and how it might engage yet further.

When this information is distilled into judgements, as in the examples above, it will form a strong position from which the school can begin to develop its thinking and plan its action. This is the time for strategy development.

Next steps: developing a strategy for action
By the time you have gathered information about what you are already doing in school, ideas will already be forming, and the strategy will already be evolving. This is human nature – we are always thinking of solutions, and it is tempting to jump ahead to put practical steps in

place when we see them. It is worth taking time to think more, however, before planning your strategy, so that it can be better informed, more comprehensive and more likely to succeed. This doesn't mean that a strategy, once formed, becomes a binding and limited plan of action, with no scope for experimentation – this won't work, not least because although we can draw together ideas and best practice developed so far on how to improve social and global mobility, one of the central aims of this vision of Powerful Schools is to find out what happens when we put these ideas into practice:

- How well do these ideas work when they are put into practice?
- What else do we discover when we try them out?
- What other ideas do these explorations prompt?

Constant evaluation and reflection will inevitably lead to a regular readjustment of strategy, and this readjustment is usually a positive sign of evolution. The next steps in developing a strategy are therefore most usefully:

- find out more about your stakeholders, and work out how and when you might engage them more effectively, including in specific stakeholder-focused audits;
- decide which areas of activity you want to prioritise, over which time period, within your boundaries of time, cost (and courage);
- develop strategies for practical action and feed these into your strategic school development plan so that they become an integral part of your annual strategic school development.

*****

You now know who your stakeholders are and what you are doing already in school and in the spheres of your school's activity to develop social and global mobility. The next step is to find out more about your stakeholders, and what motivates them. Who are they, what might make them work more closely with you on this vision, and what might they contribute?

Chapter 5

Motivations and contribution – why your stakeholders will get involved and what they can bring

In order to engage the stakeholders in schools, it is useful first to understand in more detail:

- what their potential motivations are for becoming engaged in the Powerful Schools Vision, *ie* what they might gain; and
- what they might be able to contribute if they become engaged.

Every person has a different combination of motivations that run through their lives, and these motivations will develop and change in response to all the varied circumstances of that person's life. We should never lose sight of this when making summary judgements about groups of people, especially as one of the core drivers of social and global mobility is to enable greater choice for individuals. Any overview needs to be preceded by this caveat, although it is still useful to think in broad terms about groups of people and their potential motivations, because this can give insights which can prompt creative thinking about strategies to engage them and others.

SPHERE 1: The individual

Whether they realise it or not at the outset of their education and their exposure to the 'what' and 'how' of social and global mobility, students will without doubt be the most immediate beneficiaries of a society which has more scope for social and global mobility. Students have the most to gain because the focus of schools is primarily on them, and they will be the main beneficiaries of the greater awareness, greater robustness and confidence, and greater opportunities that programmes designed to aid social and global mobility will create. They are the people who will benefit most from an increase in choice and in different pathways in society more generally.

Students are not just beneficiaries: they have the potential to be great contributors too. They can bring immense qualities to the pursuit of a goal such as social and global mobility, and will be far from passive recipients. When engaged and inspired, young people are immensely creative thinkers, and are unafraid of action if they are empowered and enabled to do so. They can also be powerful voices with other stakeholders.

Any individual person who works with the Powerful Schools Vision can be touched and affected by it personally – not just students. They may, for example, be inspired themselves to personal action when they develop greater awareness through access to some of the thinking around social and global mobility; or when they observe or contribute to some of the programmes for skills development and/or action in practice, they may be inspired to find and follow a similar programme for themselves (coaching, perhaps, or careers counselling). Anyone can gain from this personally by reassessing their life (and their family's life) within the context of the possibilities that greater social and global mobility bring. Teachers may become emboldened and decide to apply for a teaching role abroad, or local business owners may develop the confidence to reach out to different markets. Anyone who comes into contact with the Powerful Schools Vision can be impacted by it.

Equally, individual people can contribute to the vision in a myriad of ways, depending on their circumstances. In fact, action usually comes down to individuals rather than groups – even if groups decide that action is a good thing, and set out parameters for it, it will come down to individuals to make it happen. It is important to bear this in mind when considering the groups of people in the following sections – they are all composed of individuals. Insights into the motivations of the groups, and into their capacity to contribute, are just broad brushstrokes, but these insights are useful because they can help school leaders envisage how they might approach people and organisations and engage them in contributing to a wider vision of social and global mobility, driven by the school.

With this in mind, we can look at the other spheres of a school's activity, and consider what the stakeholders within them might have to gain, and to offer.

SPHERE 2: The school community

Staff, parents and school volunteers, including school board members, all have regular, direct and active connections with schools. They are part of the immediate organisation of the school – in practical terms, they actually form the school, because schools are not just buildings or organisational structures, but rather are co-constructed by the people who live, work and learn in them. What holds these people together as the school community is a set of ideas and expectations, which are converted into action, consciously or subconsciously, by individuals. This is why leadership is so crucial in schools: at its best, it will consolidate ideas and expectations into a cohesive vision, and this will shape the activity of the school. In effect, great leadership sets or clarifies a vision, and will help facilitate the connections that will allow the immediate stakeholders in the school both to understand this direction, and to translate it into action. If the leadership of the school has a clear, consistent, ambitious vision, this will form the basis of change, but it must always have regard to the motivations of individual people and groups of stakeholders.

Teachers care about students and their futures. Most teachers came into education – and remain in education – largely because they want to do something that matters for young people. They also care about being employed in an organisation which is fair and just, and where their work is fulfilling, and all of these are powerful motivations for engagement in a vision of greater social and global mobility for all.

Teachers know their students extremely well, and will be key in helping the students to understand the value of greater social and global mobility, and in enabling them to make the most of the opportunities that arise for them from it. Conversely, if they don't believe in it, or are unconvinced, this will undermine the message to students and others in the spheres of the school's activity. Some teachers – those ready for their next professional challenge – can take on key leadership roles in the strategy. There are invariably excellent creative thinkers and problem-solvers amongst staff, too, who will be able to develop innovative ideas and practices. Other teachers will be strong voices with students. The more teachers who are involved, the more consistent and cohesive the message will be to the whole school community.

Just like teachers, **non-teaching staff** too care about students and their futures. They also care about being employed in an organisation which is fair and just, and where their work is fulfilling. They often feel less connected with the school, and/or less valued than teachers, but just like teachers, they can take on key roles in the strategy, including helping organise action and programmes, and can be an equally strong and supportive voice.

School boards and governing bodies care about the school and want it and the students to be successful. They also care about the sustainable future of the school. When engaged and fully in agreement with the vision and direction of the school, they can support schools principally through decisions about the allocation of resources. They can also connect schools with external agencies and people of influence, and will add to the bank of strong and cohesive voices.

Parents/immediate carers have an obvious motivation for supporting a vision of Powerful Schools, because they care about their children and want the best for them and their future. Some parents can become very involved in the school, while others prefer an arm's length relationship, but this diversity can still be tapped: parents are a very diverse group with connections that extend far beyond the school and with a potential for far-reaching influence and very practical offers of help.

Volunteers in school, other than parents, have already demonstrated by their willingness to volunteer that they care about the school and are keen to be involved. They will have a variety of motivations for this – a social and/or philanthropic motivation, or personal enjoyment, or perhaps they have a professional obligation to carry out community service. Whatever their motivation, however, they bring time and different perspectives to schools, because volunteers often have significant lives beyond school, and access to these networks can potentially be of immense use to the school.

SPHERE 3: The local community

The local community is a particularly rich source of support for schools in their pursuit of a vision of developing greater social and global mobility for their students and for society more generally. In every local community – which can be defined as broadly as you wish – there are generally people of all ages, often from a wide variety of backgrounds, with different histories and perspectives on the world, and different networks, skills and experience which, if harnessed, can bring depth and insight to young people in school, as well as providing the base for support of the vision in a wider society. Different people – and organisations such as charities and businesses, who have the power of organisational structures behind them too – will be able to contribute to the vision in many different ways, and the huge advantage that they all possess is a physical proximity to the school. They can, if needed, come into the school in person, and this means that the scope exists to create deeper personal relationships with them.

Wider families, including grandparents, have a connection with students in the school and care about their futures. It may be more tenuous a connection than that of parents and immediate carers, and will vary enormously, depending on the family circumstances, but there is nonetheless a personal connection, and an enormously valuable one. Families vary hugely in their make-up, but each student in school will in most cases be connected through family to a network of other family members. They may live locally or far away, and they may be emotionally close or distant; nonetheless, they are still connected. These connections are worth exploring in an attempt to bring more breadth and depth of knowledge into school, and to create more conduits for the school to communicate outwardly, and to influence. Wider families have huge webs of connection and influence.

Depending on the experiences that **former students** have had at school, they may be very happy to continue to be involved in the work of the school, or vehemently opposed to it, or place themselves somewhere in between. Whatever their feelings about the school, however, or wherever they now live (which may not be at all local), the school was still a significant part of their early life, and at least a proportion of former students will have a sense of gratitude for this, and a sense of responsibility that they should 'give back' by contributing to the work of the school today, and to the life chances of current students. (This is a sense which tends to develop over time, with greater social awareness and wisdom.)

Former students will be an enormously varied group, with different ages, different jobs, different life circumstances and different perspectives on the world. This makes them a hugely rich source of adults who, if connected with current students, can help them see and appreciate a wide range of opportunities in the world. Former students, if engaged, can also help as advocates of the vision, and as catalysts in their own right for change in their fields.

Community groups, including charities and voluntary groups, care about society. Depending on the community group or charity, they may have particular links with the school, and while they are often overstretched and understaffed – and, in the case of charities, limited by the terms of their charitable goals – at some level, most charities have an aspect of their activity or potential activity which is related to social (and therefore by extension global) mobility. If it can be demonstrated to them how the Powerful Schools Vision supports their own aims, they can become very useful partners. Partnership and greater reach is essentially what these groups have to bring to the Vision. They may also be able to provide practical opportunities to develop work-related skills through volunteering, and they may be able to spread the word about the vision.

Local businesses, whether small, medium or large, offer direct access to the workplace. They operate in regulatory frameworks which young people will have to learn about in due course, and they provide examples of what work can look like. The other, very relevant, point about local businesses is that they often directly engage with national and international communities via the internet, media and social media. A small technology company, based locally, may be writing software for use on another continent; a local shop may have a mail order offshoot which sends its products across the country. Large companies, based locally or with some representation locally, may have satellite offices across the world, but a business does not now have to be large to be globally connected. These businesses have a social obligation – which most recognise at some level – to contribute to the development of young people, and they have a wider economic motivation to protect the future of their businesses (and the economy more generally) by ensuring that young people are flexible and ready to make choices in the workplace.

What hampers the engagement of businesses in investing time and resources in young people is the lack of immediate payback for businesses – *ie* if they spend time talking to students in school, or offering work experience placements and training young people in their business, it is more likely than not that this time and effort will not translate directly into one of these particular young people becoming an employee: there is not usually an direct reward. However, the fundamental point remains that if businesses can work directly with schools, young people develop social mobility because their understanding of the opportunities available to them in the world develops, and they also start to develop some of the skills they will need in order to be successful. If every company did this, so that every young person had multiple opportunities to develop work-readiness and business-awareness, the chances are that a company which invested in this would reap the rewards in an employee at a later stage who had experienced something similar as part of this wider programme. This has to be a motivating factor for businesses; in much the same way that they pay taxes which pay for emergency services, road lights and rubbish collection, investing in young people and their social opportunities will pay off. Businesses have an enormous amount to offer schools – and a motivation to do so.

Local government and local education departments are often very focused on the delivery of measurables – participation in education, exam results, career destinations and so on – and on the day-to-day administration of schools. They are also often hampered by tight budgets. All of this can make innovation harder for them, even though their prime motivation should be the development of young people in every respect, and even though, too, they are usually peopled by many staff who really want to make a positive difference, and whose goal is to encourage schools to work more smartly and boldly in pursuit of success for young people. If local government and local education departments can appreciate the value of the Powerful Schools Vision, however, they can contribute tremendous support, including resources (time and money), and a platform which enables access to other schools and to potential partnerships. Moreover, politicians who operate within these departments (as opposed to the civil servants) can often wield particular influence, and bring different perspectives which can help overcome constraints such as budgets. They can be useful allies in helping to get things done, although probably the best allies are experienced civil servants who also share a desire to make change happen, because they know how to do this, and can be very inventive in accessing the resources needed.

Further education institutions have a particularly keen interest in social mobility (which should bring with it a keen interest too in global mobility, although, again, this is not yet part of the common language around social mobility): the focus of many further education courses tends towards the vocational, and because there is generally a much greater age spread than in schools, from 16 year olds to students in their eighties, nineties and beyond, further education institutions have the ability to reach out to many groups of people, and many levels of society. People choose to study at further education institutions either because the structures of school do not suit them, or because they are too old for school; they are also usually motivated by a job-related focus, either studying to access higher education (in order to change career or just to improve their general job prospects), or studying for vocational qualifications of some kind. It therefore follows that further education institutions should – if they, like local government, can overcome their issues of tight budgets, a funding-driven need to compete for students, and focus on administration – be very sympathetic to the Powerful

Schools Vision, and willing to work closely in partnership with schools in helping to deliver it.

Only local communities know who their **local people of influence** are. These may be local politicians, local church or community leaders, or local business people. In practice, however, every single adult is a person who has some influence with others – anyone who has ever built up a relationship with anyone else has the potential to exert influence. This group is a subsection of a final locally based stakeholder group, namely that of **other adults who live locally**. These local adults (who are not parents) often feel very disconnected from schools. Even adults who are parents do not normally feel connected with schools other than the school attended by their child or children. While parents and other close family relatives have an obvious reason to engage with schools, so do too other adults (whether they realise it as yet or not), and in fact, their contribution to the school will be vital in order to further the aim of working towards social and global mobility. Every adult in our society – whether or not they have children themselves – will depend at some point in their lives on the children of today: it is these children who will grow into the careworkers, the doctors, the service providers, the gas engineers, the policymakers and the wealth creators. It is firmly in the interest of all adults – parent or not – to help ensure that young people are steered appropriately so that they become well-balanced and fulfilled adults who understand their wider responsibility for social and global development, and who act accordingly.

We all have a responsibility for bringing up our children, after all – this is a fundamental social drive. This motivation is latent in a competitive society, and has been squashed over successive decades by a focus on the individual rather than on social responsibility, but it is nonetheless still present, and this is the motivation that schools must highlight and draw on if they are to capture the skills, experience and opportunities that other adults who live locally – whether or not they are also local people of influence – can bring to schools. These adults may fall into other stakeholder groups, including businesses and community groups, but as individuals they also have immense life experience and voices which can help support the school in its pursuit of this vision. They can bring practical help by contributing to the programmes run by the school to support its students, and they can use their voices to spread the word, be this in the local supermarket, in local government, on the local 'celebrity scene', or simply with other adults.

SPHERE 4: the national community

The national community is significant in two ways – it provides access to, and a means to communicate with, a collection of local communities which in practice make up the national community, but it also has a life and existence of its own, as an entity which makes decisions about matters which affect the whole nation. Both of these are significant and of interest to Powerful Schools. In seeking to work with and influence the national community, schools are in part seeking to access very local communities and school communities so as to spread the word and help them to work actively on a school-centred vision for engaging society in developing greater social and global mobility. In part, too, they are seeking to establish a national understanding of, and approval for, the Powerful Schools Vision. The more national legitimacy any policy has, the easier it is to get things done, and the more funding is likely to become available to help make it happen. Even though this is a vision which can and should be embedded in schools and led by them, there are some obvious advantages to gaining national approval.

Like local government, **national government** bodies are often constrained by budgets and measurable targets, but they are also still motivated by the desire to develop greater social and global mobility. They see the economic value in enabling young people to have greater opportunities through social and global mobility, as they can become a more fluid and more effective workforce, contributing to a greater economic impact, and they are generally able to articulate this more effectively than local government because they have a greater remit, and greater access to funds and partnerships in order to make this happen. They have, in fact, significant power – not least legislative power – to make things happen.

Similarly, **national businesses** also often have a wider remit than local businesses, and often have access to greater funds. They can be motivated by a desire to achieve greater political approval, and/or because their directors and shareholders value social action, and/or because there are financial incentives; any or all of these motivations can be powerful for businesses with a national reach. Like national government bodies, national businesses have a significant ability to access and use resources such as time and money – and connections and networks – to support schools in very practical ways.

People of national influence include both the visible and the invisible – people who are in the public eye, and whose words are listened to and reported on by the media, as well as people who are trusted, and listened to, by decision-makers in politics and business. These are all people who can make a difference if they are public and vocal supporters of the vision of Powerful Schools, or if they introduce the vision to people who can help implement some of the practicalities that will make it come to fruition.

National organisations – whether charities, support groups, political groups, lobbying groups or any other group – all have a stake in society. They should care about social development and growth, and about making a change for the better. Their potential contribution to a schools-based vision of developing greater social and global mobility will vary enormously, depending on their principal goals and how they are constituted, as well as the resources to which they have access, but there is no doubt that they can be powerful allies.

Universities have come under notable pressure in the past few years to demonstrate that they are contributing to social mobility, and they would almost certainly argue strongly that not only do they do this, but that they contribute significantly to global mobility too – most universities are extremely international institutions, with international students and staff, and overseas partnerships. For them, it makes enormous sense to be able to support the work of schools to develop social and global mobility at a younger age, because this will take some of the pressure from them, and it will enable them to focus better on their core academic activity. They have an enormous amount to contribute to the Powerful Schools Vision, including opportunities for young people to work with older students, to access the networks that universities have built up, and to work on research methodology that will support the drive towards greater social and global mobility.

SPHERE 5: *The international community*

We mustn't lose sight of the fact that, just as the national community is a collection of local communities, so too is the international community a collection of national communities, and through them local communities. However – again, just like the national community – the international community has a life of its own, evident in organisations (including governmental organisations like the EU, the UN and multiple other international governmental alliances) which cross national borders and work internationally. Dealing with 'the international community' therefore brings with it a number of possibilities on a spectrum of opportunities, from building a personal and professional partnership with a school abroad, or reaching out to share cultural ties with organisations based in other countries, or from planning international work experience for students with a multi-national corporation to reading about best practice from wider networks (*eg* UNESCO projects), and contributing in turn to these networks to spread the best practice in programmes developed in school to support social and global mobility.

The motivations for engagement by **people of international influence** will depend enormously on the person; what is striking about people who have some kind of influence in our society, however, is that they often have a very strong commitment and desire to make a positive difference in the world, and they can bring a range of often very significant resources and connections. People who have international influence include people in the public eye and those behind the scenes – what matters is that they have the means to contribute in numerous ways, including providing access to those who have the ability to make a global impact.

International governmental organisations want the same as most national and local governmental organisations – at the heart of their activity sits equality of human beings, and respect for others, as made explicit in the UN's 1948 Universal Declaration of Human Rights. They have many other pressing roles, too – trying to maintain global security through diplomacy and other means, and preventing the world from destroying itself – but the empowerment of individuals so that they have the opportunity to become equal is one of the most powerful central motivating drives at the core of international governmental activity. Social and global mobility matter at an international level – they are the answer to eliminating poverty and hunger, and they are embedded in thinking about how to develop effective programmes. As such international organisations – and the non-governmental international organisations (NGOs) such as **international charities** which work with them – are entrusted with public money, their capacity for experimentation and risk-taking is limited – they want to know that a programme works, that it offers good value for money and, that it is measurable, scalable and sustainable. The Powerful Schools Vision, as it develops, will however almost certainly be of real interest to them, because it reflects already some of the work that is going on in schools around the world, and it has the potential to make a huge difference to future generations.

International governmental organisations, therefore, are a huge resource for schools, and a prime source of information and knowledge about successful programmes that already contribute to social and global mobility. They can also make things happen on a large scale, albeit it often in a steady and measured way. (The significant impact of the Millennium Development Goals over the 15 year period from 2000 to 2015 is evidence of this.) Moreover, international government works because it creates partnerships with national governments and other organisations, and its reach is enormous. Access to these partnerships, knowledge and experience is of immense value to schools. Rather than feeling daunted by the remoteness of international government and the machinery it has built around it to make things happen on a global scale, they should be inspired by the focus of international government on local impact, and feel a degree of entitlement to access – after all, what Powerful Schools have to offer fits very much within the remit of international government.

All **international organisations, including businesses**, have connections, far-reaching networks, and the ability to make more connections and have an impact in different parts of the world. Some will have a greater interest than others in, and focus on, social and global mobility as a concept and a driving factor, and some will be more open than others to partnering with schools in seeking to help develop this social and global mobility. They may have different levels of motivation to help effect social change (and different reasons for this motivation), different strategic priorities, different capacities for action and different degrees of willingness for engagement, but the scope is there for schools to align themselves with the motivations of a number of international organisations, and through them to achieve wider reach and impact.

EXERCISE: Can you think of any other motivating factors for your stakeholders? And what else do you think they might bring to your school, and the vision you are developing of a Powerful School? The more you can understand what motivates your stakeholders, the easier it will be to align what you want to do with what they are interested in and motivated by, so it is worth spending time doing this. Note down what you think motivates them, and make a point of thinking more about this, and delving deeper, as you engage more with them.

Stakeholders	What would motivate them to help the school develop into a more Powerful School, focused on social and global mobility?	What could they contribute to this process of becoming a more Powerful School, focused on social and global mobility?
Students		
Teachers		
Non-teaching staff		
Volunteers in school		
School boards		
Parents/carers		
Grandparents/wider families		
Former students		
Community groups – charities, voluntary groups, different age sectors		
Businesses – small, medium, large		
Universities and further education institutions		
Government – local, national, international		
National organisations – charities/support groups/ political groups/lobbying groups		
People of influence – local, national, international		
International relationships – organisations, businesses, movements		

Connecting across the spheres of activity – schools and networks of schools

In practice, other schools can be found in every sphere of a Powerful

School's activity. Individual personal relationships between local schools abound – between their Heads, their senior leaders and their staff, as well as between students, parents and many other stakeholder groups. Schools have multiple professional relationships too with other schools, perhaps because they sit within the same local communities – the same governmental organisation, maybe – or because they are run by the same education group, or because they participate in the same professional networks, from local clusters to national organisations such as teacher support associations. Through these wider local and national (and sometimes international) networks, too, they have the ability to learn from and to influence one another, sharing insights, thinking and best practice, and working together on projects. Many schools have several connections with schools in different countries, and have built successful and sustained relationships with them. Schools are very, very connected with one another, in many, different ways – not least through their shared purpose. Although they are often in competition (for the recruitment of students and staff, for funds, and for a position at the top of school league tables), when schools collaborate, it makes much, much more possible – after all, no one school can provide for the needs of all of society's children. The potential impact of all schools speaking with one voice is powerful to imagine.

The motivations for all schools to get involved in developing a greater vision of social and global mobility are essentially the same (as, indeed, are the elements that get in the way – see Chapter 1 – which we must not forget). A shared motivation and commitment to developing greater and social mobility means that schools together are stronger. When other schools buy into and become involved in the Powerful Schools Vision, then the potential impact of the vision is multiplied. Morcover, when the ideas, inspirations and innovations which come out of another school's activity are pooled and shared, the scope for even greater and more effective action grows: it is often easier for schools to pick from a range of tried-and-tested programmes and approaches than it is to develop their own. The sharing of good practice is a great advantage that collaboration between schools brings, and when this is multiplied across the many relationships that schools have with other schools, and across all the networks – local, national and global – with which they connect, then the potential for significant global impact is enormous.

EXERCISE: Think about all the relationships your school has with other schools. Where might you place these schools in the spheres of activity below?

	Which schools are you connected with?	How are you connected with them?
Individual		
School community		
Local community		
National community		
International community		

What does this tell you about your relationships with other schools? Where are your strongest relationships, where you might start when you begin to reach out to other schools? With which schools might you want to develop further relationships for the future? What can you find out about the schools with which you have relationships? Are any of them already working on developing social and global mobility? If so, how can you connect with them?

*****

This question of <u>how</u> you engage with your stakeholders is the most pressing one now. You have a sense of what you are already doing in school to help develop social and global mobility, and you also have a sense of who your stakeholders are, and what might motivate them to get involved with your school as part of the vision of schools at the heart of developing social and global mobility. The next big question now is ... how do you engage your stakeholders?

Chapter 6

How do you engage your stakeholders? Realms of powerful activity

In a similar model to that of the activity of Powerful Schools, it is possible to create a model of types of powerful activity, radiating out from a core of personal relationships, and the possibilities for activity, action and influence that this brings. These 'realms of powerful activity' can actually become more meaningful in enabling action than simply the spheres of activity identified earlier – *ie* the areas in which schools operate, because these 'realms' focus principally on what schools can do in order to make change happen:

A. The power of personal relationships.

The strongest human relationships are usually personal ones. These relationships are built through direct, regular and personal connection, and through working closely together with a shared purpose. The most obvious people with whom personal relationships can be built are students and staff, but depending on the leadership style of senior leaders, and their particular experiences and connections, this could also include parents, members of the community, and even politicians and people in positions of responsibility at key partner institutions and organisations (*eg* universities and/or local or national businesses). The key defining feature of this group is that they have a personal connection with the school, and with the school leaders in particular – they will most likely be aligned already with the values of the school, and open to being inspired to action. They will contribute to the Powerful Schools Vision because they trust the school leadership and because they feel the leaders care about them.

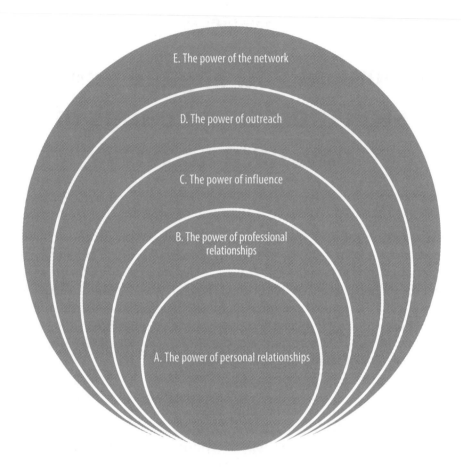

E. The power of the network

D. The power of outreach

C. The power of influence

B. The power of professional relationships

A. The power of personal relationships

B. *The power of professional relationships*

After personal relationships, professional relationships are probably some of the strongest relationships that a school can build. These relationships are founded on a mutual contract of some kind – formal or informal – which binds the school and other organisations or individuals in a joint working relationship. People and organisations in a professional relationship with a school will have different degrees of engagement with the school, but they nonetheless, because of the mutually beneficial nature of their relationship, all have a strong vested interest in the success of schools. They do however expect the school to work for them as well as with them. The most obvious people to whom this applies are teachers, and other stakeholders in the school community, but line managers at local government or school board level sit within this realm too. This group could also include other adults who learn at the school (in evening classes, for instance), or other organisations which connect with the school in some way (*eg* charities which run work experience programmes). Some students will also fall into this category – those students in particular who are less convinced of the value of school, perhaps, or those who are appropriately sceptical and who need convincing about the value of engagement. The key defining feature of this group is that their engagement with the school is not unconditional – it is conditional on a number of factors, based on rational expectations and a clear understanding of mutual benefit.

C. The power of influence

Influencing is a step further away still from personal relationships, and it can be hard. In the context of powerful schools, essentially it involves establishing a relationship of trust with others, often through third parties, where no or only a tenuous (or passive) relationship previously existed. This new relationship must be strong enough to ensure that the stakeholders concerned will become active in the cause of the Powerful Schools Vision. Influence is a significant factor in most relationships, and therefore runs through all the spheres of activity of a school's work: strong and lasting personal relationships with individuals are built on trust rather than coercion, and influence is central to these relationships; equally, outreach and working through networks could perhaps be described as extended influence. Key, core principles underpin successful influencing, and these are worth returning to as a checklist when planning how to interact with all the school's stakeholders:

- be authentic: believe in the vision and live it;
- lead with integrity.

This realm of powerful activity includes people who are not usually involved in everyday school activities, but who are likely to be connected with the school in some, either through physical proximity or because they have an interest in the school (perhaps because they know students or teachers who are part of the school), or because a relationship has been built with them in the past that has led them to become more closely involved in an aspect of school life (mentoring, for example, or providing work experience). This is a group with whom the leadership of the school may be able to connect directly and personally, but (in part because to do so would be likely to stretch the workload capacity available in school) is in practice much more likely to be drawn into the work of the school through people who are members of the school community – students, perhaps, or teachers – and will do so because the school has succeeded in positively influencing people to believe in and engage in the Powerful Schools Vision.

D. The power of outreach

In today's technologically connected world, it is easier than ever to disseminate information, ideas and opinions, and to reach out so that other people can see what you are doing and what you are thinking. The sheer amount of information that is generated every day, however, means that it is not sufficient simply to imagine that by stating or telling people what you are doing, they will change their thinking, or contribute in some way to what you are seeking to do. People are looking for trusted information and a connection with their core activity and interests; any strategy involving outreach which is not based on these elements will most likely fail.

Areas to consider in developing further relationships in this realm of activity:

- Build a robust digital presence around the Powerful Schools Vision, as this is how, increasingly, people connect with institutions and come to trust them:
  - Make sure your website has a dedicated page about the Vision, updated regularly with news on what you are doing
  - Build a social media strategy so that you can communicate what you are doing, and why, in a simple, clear and regular way. Effective social media engagement cannot be an afterthought – it has to be planned and implemented.
- Ensure that external messaging around the Powerful Schools Vision is clear, cohesive, targeted and relentless.

- Build relationships of trust with people who can in turn take the ideas to other people.
- Track engagement with people and groups, and map this regularly against your desired spheres of activity – this will help you frame messaging to retain interest from existing engaged groups and to generate interest from groups which you want to target.

This realm of powerful activity is in many ways the most challenging to capture, because it can be the most distant (although as pointed out in Chapter 3, there can be many cross-overs between groups in the form of, for example, parents). However, because this group overlaps with many of the national stakeholders, who have national influence and power, it often also has the greatest potential to adopt the ideas of the Powerful Schools Vision and propagate them on a wider plane, thus helping bring the vision to fruition in a way that a single school (or indeed group of schools) cannot achieve on its own. Building personal relationships with some of the stakeholder groups in this realm of activity can help (and therefore in effect convert them into members of the first realm of activity), but it is entirely impractical to imagine that the stakeholder groups listed in this section can all be converted into close relationships, or even be influenced by members of the school community. These groups need to be won over and engaged through other means than by reaching out and connecting directly.

E. The power of the network

No one school can connect with everyone. The world is too big and too complex for that to be viable; moreover, this is not a vision for a Powerful School, but a vision of all schools as Powerful Schools. This is why collaboration with other schools is so important, and why the networks that are built up through other organisations are so necessary, so that others can engage with their stakeholders through personal and professional relationships, and can influence and reach out to them. Where the real power of the network lies, of course, is in the 'power of the crowd' – the more schools which buy into a vision that schools can be powerful generators of social and global mobility, and the more schools there are which work, actively, to bring this vision to fruition, the more, together, they will change understandings locally, nationally and globally of what schools can and should be doing in this field. The more schools who are doing it, and the more connected they are in the clarity of their vision, the more other people are going to listen, accept, adopt and engage.

In very broad terms, and as is obvious from the descriptions above, these 'realms of powerful activity' can be seen to correlate roughly with the five spheres of activity of a Powerful School. It makes practical sense to attribute to each sphere the most likely approach that the school will adopt in seeking to engage its members. Realms of powerful activity are not restricted to spheres of a school's activity, and grouping stakeholders according to a proposed methodology of action can make the task of future engagement easier to conceptualise for schools, which can mean that it is more likely to lead to effective action. When the 'who' and the 'how' are intertwined, action often seems far easier, and if the school understands from the outset how it can connect most powerfully with these groups, it is far more likely to be able to develop the strategies needed to do so. If each sphere of activity therefore effectively overlaps with a 'realm of powerful activity', denoting them as such in practice is empowering for schools, because it makes action seem possible.

EXERCISE: Look again at the list of your stakeholders in Chapter 3. Think about HOW you engage with them, specifically in order to help make change happen. Where would you place them in the five realms of powerful activity in the following table? Don't wrestle with this too much – while you will draw on the information you have gathered in the initial audit, use your own personal experience too. Be specific rather than general, though, and don't hesitate to split groups of stakeholders across the different realms of influence – stakeholder groups are not homogenous entities, after all. It is entirely to be expected that you will have stronger and weaker relationships with individual stakeholders or sub-groups of stakeholders within one of the groups identified earlier. Not all students are the same (far from it!), nor are all teachers, or parents *etc.* You may, for example, have strong, personal relationships with colleagues in one university, and a very distant relationship with another institution, with which you may in fact connect only through a network.

In filling in your impressions in the table below, you can name these sub-groups so that you know exactly to what you are referring (*eg* University X, Universities Y and Z):

HOW DO YOU ENGAGE WITH YOUR STAKEHOLDERS?	WHICH STAKEHOLDERS DO YOU ENGAGE WITH IN THIS WAY?
A. Through personal relationships	
B. Through professional relationships	
C. Through influence	
D. Through outreach	
E. Through a network	

This exercise provides you with an alternative way of grouping your stakeholders. The value that comes from this kind of analysis lies in how it can help you and your team or teams in school to think about how you already engage with your stakeholders, how you might engage better with them, and which strategies you want to prioritise.

*****

The next step, then, is to look at each stakeholder group in turn and to work out how to engage them effectively in the Powerful Schools Vision. Developing the awareness of stakeholders and involving them in practical action: these are driving forces in Chapter 7.

Chapter 7

Building the power: practical ideas to engage stakeholder groups

How this chapter is organised

For ease of reference, this chapter looks at the stakeholders in school in the same order (and grouped according to the same sphere of activity) as is followed in the earlier chapters of this book. Each section stands alone, however, so you can read them in any order. In order to make the section on each stakeholder group effective as a standalone source of ideas and action, each section is also prefaced by a table that prompts a mini self-evaluation. This self-evaluation is obviously going to be more effective if it draws together insights you have already gathered as part of an auditing process and your own reflection and thinking, based on the ideas explored in this book, but it does also mean that each of these sections can be treated in isolation, as individual areas of focus, if you decide that your strategy in school is only to focus on engaging particular stakeholder groups. Obviously, the more groups you engage, the more effective the overall impact, and the more the groups will be able to influence one another and enhance each other's effectiveness, but schools have to decide for themselves how to do this. Different schools will go about this drive towards enabling a vision for greater social and global mobility in different ways.

Self-evaluation:

What is the school already doing to raise the awareness of (this stakeholder group) about social and global mobility?	What is the school already doing to involve (this stakeholder group) in practical action and/or skills development?
What does or should motivate (this stakeholder group) to get more involved in developing the school's vision of social and global mobility?	What can (this stakeholder group) contribute to the vision of developing social and global mobility?
How is the school engaging with (this stakeholder group) (eg through personal relationships, professional relationships, through influence, through outreach, and/or through a network)?	To what extent is the school really engaged with (this stakeholder group)? How could the school become better engaged with (this stakeholder group)?

Self-evaluation is the foundation of change, and leads to the thinking that will lead to the action that you will take, and that will be specific to your particular school and the unique combination of circumstances in which your school finds itself. The ideas and thoughts that accompany the self-evaluation for each stakeholder group in this chapter are only ideas, and in some cases only scratch the surface of what can be achieved in schools. Your school will almost certainly be engaged already in many of the activities identified, and you may well be a leader in your field already. Ask yourself the following questions as you consider how to move forward:

- What else can we do to develop social and global mobility for our students and more widely?
- How can we extend what we already offer so that every single student has a rich and varied set of opportunities?
- How can we engage more people in what we are doing?
- How can we strengthen and extend our influence so that schools really do become powerful engines of social and global mobility?

The ideas and examples given are not designed to be a prescription for your particular school. They are gathered together in order to start the process of sharing good practice and to prompt your thinking and the thinking of your stakeholders. Read them with this in mind.

The individual student (Sphere 1, at the heart of the school's activity)

What is the school already doing to raise the awareness of students about social and global mobility?	What is the school already doing to involve students in practical action and/or skills development?
What does or should motivate students to get more involved in developing the school's vision of social and global mobility?	What can students contribute to the vision of developing social and global mobility?
How is the school engaging with students (eg through personal relationships, professional relationships, through influence, through outreach, and/or through a network)?	To what extent is the school really engaged with students? How could the school become better engaged with students?

How can we find out more about students' involvement with the school's vision for social and global mobility?

Ask them! This can be informal or formal, and it might be more effective if done in conjunction with an awareness-raising programme as suggested below, so that the discussion is more informed. Class discussion, or a short questionnaire, or groupwork – any of these methods (and others) could help elicit what students already know about the school's role in developing awareness of social and global mobility with them and with other sectors of society, and also how the school works in order practically to develop social and global mobility. They may or may not recognise that some of the opportunities they are given by the school every day (*eg* to develop their personal management skills, or to develop leadership skills) are all important in developing their personal social and global mobility, and in laying the groundwork for better social and global mobility for all.

When you are quizzing students, check that they understand that you are asking them not just about the impact that a vision for social and global mobility will have on them personally, but also about the impact that the school can have on society as a whole – locally, nationally and globally – both by involving these wider sectors in what the school does and in influencing these sectors to work towards greater social and global mobility in their own areas of activity.

Record students' thoughts and make sure that these are passed on so they can be recorded centrally too, and feed into the whole school strategy. Asking these questions and prompting thinking is only the first step in recognising what is actually going on in school, and this in turn is only the first step is developing strategies that will lead to more effective action.

Ideas for raising students' awareness about social and global mobility

- Design a short lesson, or presentation, or programme of a few sessions to introduce students of different ages to the concept of social and global mobility. The more students you can deliver this to, the better – of all ages. Even very young students can start thinking about, for example, what it means to be able to choose to work at different jobs and in different places, and what we need to do in order to make friends with people from different parts of the world who know different things from us.

- Use the ideas explored earlier in this book as the basis of discussion on social and global mobility. Transmitting knowledge and understanding through the focus of a discussion has the benefit of really engaging students as stakeholders in co-creating knowledge by helping them identify for themselves what social and global mobility does or could do for them, for the school community, for the local community, for the national community, and for the international community.

- Develop opportunities to engage all students in thinking about connection, influence and power, and how what they think and do can influence the thinking and activity of their families, the local and wider groups in which they are involved, and their own networks and circles.

Ideas for involving students in practical action and/or skills development

- Extend personal development programmes which are already embedded in the curriculum, and consider involving other stakeholders in these, so that all students have regular exposure to activities in school which really contribute to their knowledge and personal development and therefore help prepare them more effectively to become successful socially and globally mobile citizens. These programmes might be fully integrated into curriculum subjects, and/or they may stand alone as in-school or out-of-school activities – trips, residential programmes *etc.* They are likely to include:

  - teamwork and leadership programmes (which most schools do extremely well), and opportunities to put these into practice – to work as teams and to take on positions of responsibility. These are likely to include programmes focused on community service and volunteering.

  - life skills – financial awareness, what to be aware of when you travel, laws and regulations, national and international politics, current and international affairs *etc.*

  - character-building – resilience, optimism, grit, mental toughness, emotional security, self-confidence, self-esteem, self-awareness, spiritual development *etc.*

  - critical, creative, flexible and adaptable thinking, as well as ethical and moral development.

- Extend existing opportunities for students to develop an awareness of options for future study and careers, and again consider involving other stakeholders. Think about how you could extend access to younger students and how you could enable more students to access these opportunities more regularly. These opportunities might include:

  - a detailed careers education programme – your school will almost certainly have a thorough programme in place. How can you extend it and make it even more effective and far-reaching?

- interview skills, public speaking and debating skills, and practice in writing applications – general communication skills, in fact.

- Careers Weeks (or fortnights) where the explicit focus in school is on understanding the workplace, and where all students have opportunities to hear from people who are currently working about what they do, to visit workplaces, to start exploring personal thoughts and ideas for the future, and so on.

- meaningful work experience, with detailed preparation in school ahead of the experience, and a thorough debrief afterwards, to maximise the learning.

- work shadowing opportunities at all ages, from visits to factories which take children through all the processes needed to produce a food item, to a week spent with a lawyer, sitting in on meetings and experiencing the variety of tasks involved in a single job.

- enterprise programmes, including setting up and running a company, using an initial small financial stake to design and sell a new product and make a profit, and hearing from successful entrepreneurs.

- Extend existing opportunities for students to develop cultural awareness and an international or global mindset, and again consider involving other stakeholders. Think about how you could extend access to younger students and how you could enable more students to access these opportunities more regularly. These opportunities might include:

  - bringing local faith groups into school and arranging visits out of school, so that students can see and understand the different cultures present in their local vicinity.

  - organising celebrations of different cultures in school, either on a rolling basis or during a focused week or fortnight. This could include 'Culture Week', 'World Week', or 'Asia Week'; different classes could research and prepare information, skills, language, cuisine *etc* from different countries, and share it with others. Primary schools, with their interdisciplinary topic focuses, are often extremely good at this kind of approach, and the learning that results can be exceptional; it can be harder to accomplish this in secondary schools, which tend towards individual subject focuses, in preparation for external examinations, but this kind of learning is potentially very rich indeed, and should not be dismissed out of hand as 'for children'.

- arranging visits to the school from groups from abroad, and planning them well so that students can genuinely interact. When students are able to work with other students on a joint project – of any length or on any topic – this is when they really begin to collaborate, and learn about one another as they do so. Such projects can usefully be the central focus of any school visit.

- organising visits, school exchanges and work experience abroad. Again, when students have the opportunity to work on a meaningful joint project with their counterparts, this is when real collaboration and learning takes place, and it is worth planning. Developing a relationship with (ideally several) partner schools in different parts of the world will broaden the scope and the scale of the opportunities available to students to learn about other cultures and to feel confident dealing in and with them.

- facilitating fundraising for international charity projects, and using the opportunity to learn about the areas of the world concerned, and the particular issues that they face. This fundraising may take place solely within the school or the local community, or it may involve overseas travel; in any case, it is an excellent opportunity to engage with other stakeholder groups and to work in partnership with them, with a central focus on international affairs.

- considering using a framework such as the British Council International Schools Award to help track and extend international opportunities available to students.

- Doing and experiencing are often more powerful than just seeing or reading. Consider developing additional programmes and opportunities in each of the three areas identified immediately above – personal development programmes, careers/further study programmes and international/cultural programmes – especially if there are particular areas which you identify as less well-covered in school, or to which students have less access than you might like.

- Ensure all students achieve the best examination grades they can ... this is obvious, and it is what all schools try their utmost to achieve anyway, but given that academic achievement contributes to social and global mobility, it would be remiss to overlook it here.

A final note in this section: there are numerous examples of good practice of many of the ideas listed above – and books written about them; if you can draw these together into a rich matrix of activity which recognises the value that they bring individually and collectively to the capacity of individuals to become more socially and globally mobile, your students will benefit enormously.

Teachers (Sphere 2: the school community)

What is the school already doing to raise the awareness of teachers about social and global mobility?	What is the school already doing to involve teachers in practical action and/or skills development?
What does or should motivate teachers to get more involved in developing the school's vision of social and global mobility?	What can teachers contribute to the vision of developing social and global mobility?
How is the school engaging with teachers (eg through personal relationships, professional relationships, through influence, through outreach, and/or through a network)?	To what extent is the school really engaged with teachers? How could the school become better engaged with teachers?

How can we find out more about teachers' involvement with the school's vision for social and global mobility?

Your internal audit will hopefully tell you a lot about teachers and their interest and involvement in a vision which will lead to schools becoming more powerful in the drive for social and global mobility. The process of communicating with teachers about the internal audit may also bring to the surface teachers who have a particular passion for social and global mobility, who can then become key drivers in the move to design and implement programmes, and to connect with other stakeholder groups to harness their interest and to engage them effectively.

Ideas for raising teachers' awareness about social and global mobility

- Plan an in-school professional development session or series of sessions that explore the ideas in this book, explaining why they are important, and what schools can do in order to drive social change, by contributing to the Powerful Schools Vision.

- Use the internal audit as a launchpad for discussion and action; if the questions in the audit become embedded in the annual strategic school development cycle, and it becomes a requirement for teachers to report on the progress made in each of the areas identified in the audit, then this will maintain an awareness of social and global mobility.

- Set up research groups – Reading Rounds, perhaps – led by teachers (but which could also include other stakeholders), which meet regularly to find, share and discuss evidence that emerges worldwide about how to promote social and global mobility. The information that emerges from these research groups could be distilled into a variety of formats (*eg* poster, website, regular newsletter) to make it accessible to as wide a number of other interested stakeholders as possible.

- Emphasise – and keep emphasising – that this focus on social and global mobility is not about highlighting existing inequality, which many teachers would rightly feel to be potentially a very sensitive issue and a barrier to their personal and professional involvement in engaging with students on the subject. Discussions on social and global mobility (and practical action to promote it), if not handled within the wider scope of a vision for greater access and equality, risk identifying differences between students, whereas a strong and disciplined focus on a vision for greater mobility for all is robustly forward-looking, not backward-looking. Teachers will also – again, quite rightly – highlight the importance of external factors (especially family background) in limiting or promoting social and global mobility. What is the point of developing a raft of new opportunities, they may argue, if the students who might benefit from them most are not encouraged at home to take them up? The answer to this is that teachers have a very important role indeed in enabling students to take up opportunities (see below); the vision of greater social and global mobility will not be met if the opportunities are only available to, or taken up by, a few, and the teachers will be key in helping to make this happen. They cannot change family background, but they can focus forward and help students take up opportunities that may prove vitally important to them.

Ideas for involving teachers in practical action and/or skills development

- Support teachers in developing a personal relationship with their students. The power of a word of encouragement from a teacher to a student is so strong that it alone can literally be life-changing. Teachers who know their students (and their families) well enough to know when to encourage a student to do something that will have a positive impact on their personal or social or career or cultural development – and, importantly, who follow it up, checking that the student has done this, not letting it slide – can have a huge impact on students and the subsequent direction of their life. Just the realisation that a trusted adult believes in them and wants to encourage them can be tremendously powerful for students – far more so than teachers often appreciate at the time. By knowing their students, and knowing when to intervene to help them move from apathy or uncertainty to action and self-belief, teachers are doing something very practical which will have a direct impact on their students' future social and global mobility. This intervention may of course have an academic focus, helping students to study or revise more effectively (we must not forget that success in examinations makes a difference to social and global mobility), but it may equally be as simple as encouraging them to develop or pursue a nascent passion by coming along to a certain club or activity, or introducing them to a potential career by encouraging them to apply for a specific work experience placement, or challenging them to develop a greater confidence in international travel by encouraging them to raise sponsorship to go on one of the school's international exchanges. Each of these easy little steps can potentially lead to significant future opportunities for the students involved, and it can all come down to a word of encouragement given by a teacher. Teachers can make the most enormous difference to the lives of students, as long as they know them well and have the time to support them. Schools can help teachers do this by:

- giving ownership to teachers of a key goal in school – that by the time each student leaves compulsory education, the school will have identified and facilitated the core actions the student will need to take (and in many cases will already have taken) in order to enable him or her to take up any pathway they want to in life. If this becomes the dominant goal of everyday teacher activity, it frees teachers to shift their emphasis slightly, taking it away solely from grades and targets without diminishing the importance of these. Good grades are part of a portfolio of achievements that a student needs in order to become successfully socially and globally mobile, and this shift in emphasis recognises this.

- explicitly recognising – in guidelines for teachers and in their core job descriptions – the importance of all teacher-student relationships, not just relationships between students and the teachers or tutors who have a specific pastoral or guidance responsibility for them.

- finding ways to give teachers time to get to know their students – dedicated tutor time, smaller classes, less of an administrative burden ... these are familiar requests by teachers, and inevitably come under budgetary scrutiny, but the fact remains that the more time that teachers have to get to know their students, the more able they will be to build a solid relationship of trust, and the more likely they will be to make the right suggestion at just the right moment that could make a huge difference to that particular student's life chances.

- putting thought into how to match students with teacher-mentors who will be particularly inspiring and helpful to them. (There is no easy structural or systems answer to this, and no 'one-size-fits-all' solution. Just spending time thinking about it, however, can lead to some innovative solutions.)

- supporting teachers in their dealings with families. No teacher is going to want to reach out to families if they feel that the school will not support them if communication goes awry or if there is a complaint because the family feels that the teacher has overstepped a mark. If a teacher can feel empowered to contact a family and offer to help in making something happen for a student, however, this can be extremely powerful. Schools can help by offering guidelines and training for contacting families, practical support such as time, and robust tracking to make sure that all students really are benefiting from equality of access to opportunities in school.

- Make it an expectation that every teacher becomes involved in practical action. This idea will take time to embed, as you cannot develop a passion overnight in teachers who have other priorities, and success in winning teachers over will depend on your powers of influence and engagement. The more teachers you can involve in practical action, however, the stronger the school's impact can be, as a teacher is one of the school's most powerful assets, working directly with students to enhance the opportunities available to them, and with the potential too to connect – from a position of authority – with numerous external stakeholders, both in their own personal networks and in the wider networks established by the school.

- Encourage teachers to adapt their existing subject-based curricula to include specific references to how the knowledge or skills developed will help promote greater social and global mobility. The Languages Faculty has a particular role to play in this respect, by developing programmes to extend language awareness in schools. These programmes, once established, could equally benefit other stakeholder groups if run either digitally or as additional courses outside the school. They might include:

  - Language Awareness Weeks, where students experience taster lessons in a range of world languages.

  - additional language courses developed in conjunction with other local education institutions (*eg* Further Education

Colleges), aimed at different outcomes (eg basic level only, or national examination level). It is worth exploring the use of blended learning approaches to language learning, including online tutoring. These could be run as clubs or extra school courses, or even as options within the timetable.

- developing a hub of online and digital resources for more formal as well as informal language learning, connecting with successful programmes around the world.

- Use existing links with partner schools in different parts of the world (and create new links) to design detailed and meaningful opportunities for teachers' professional development. When teachers themselves become more globally aware and more confident in learning from and sharing with other cultures, they are inevitably better placed to communicate the advantages of this to their students. These opportunities might include:

  - sharing good practice with teachers in regular Skype link-ups, which could be either informal discussions or more formal involvement in seminars and professional development session. If your school has access to video-conferencing software, use it.

  - co-developing, running and evaluating programmes for students on areas where the schools' curricula overlap.

  - on-site visits to share good practice and to learn. Nothing really replaces the value of going to different countries and experiencing all aspects of life there, from weather to customs and expectations, and everything else that we take for granted in our daily lives. To make the visits (and reciprocal visits by teachers to your school) as meaningful as possible, ensure that they include at least one project of mutual benefit, which will give the visiting teacher a focus and a reason to collaborate with his/her counterparts.

- Use teachers' personal experiences – of previous careers, of international travel, of living abroad or in different parts of the country – to feed into seminar programmes, discussions and *eg* Culture Weeks or Enterprise Weeks. When teachers talk about themselves as human beings, and share experience, students listen and learn.

If the school is proactive in developing opportunities for other adults to learn and develop themselves (including language skills courses), then teachers – as well as any other adults in the local community – can benefit from these too. The development of social and global mobility should not be restricted to students – if the school genuinely is a hub of powerful activity, then it will inevitably have an impact on adults too. Teachers will gain as well as give, and this is to be welcomed.

Non-teaching staff (Sphere 2: the school community)

What is the school already doing to raise the awareness of non-teaching staff about social and global mobility?	What is the school already doing to involve non-teaching staff in practical action and/or skills development?
What does or should motivate non-teaching staff to get more involved in developing the school's vision of social and global mobility?	What can non-teaching staff contribute to the vision of developing social and global mobility?
How is the school engaging with non-teaching staff (eg through personal relationships, professional relationships, through influence, through outreach, and/or through a network)?	To what extent is the school really engaged with non-teaching staff? How could the school become better engaged with non-teaching staff?

How can we find out more about non-teaching staff's involvement with the school's vision for social and global mobility?

The internal audit will hopefully tell you something about non-teaching staff and their interest and involvement in a vision which will lead to schools becoming more powerful in the drive for social and global mobility. It might not, though – it depends on whether you have asked them directly, and to what extent they are very aware of the school's aims and how it sets about achieving them. Many non-teaching staff feel really quite distant from decision-making in the school, and many undervalue their own role in the school. They can be a hugely untapped resource in schools. To find out what they think and know about what the school can and should be doing to help its students become more socially and globally mobile, start by just asking them. How you do this is entirely up to you – through small group discussions, perhaps, or a simple questionnaire, or any other means that are most likely to elicit a thoughtful response from your particular non-teaching staff.

Ideas for raising non-teaching staff's awareness about social and global mobility

- Emphasise their importance to students and to their personal development. Non-teaching staff fulfil a variety of roles in school, from administration or servicing the school (catering, cleaning *etc*) to classroom support and student supervision (in the playground, at lunchtime, in bus queues *etc*); some of these roles involve more contact with students than others, but non-teaching staff can expect to come into direct contact with students at some point every day. Their interactions with those students, and the relationships they build with them, are important means by which they can influence young people. Besides, every role in school makes an important contribution to the effective running of the school and therefore to its vision. Everything that non-teaching staff do in school therefore adds to the overall impact of the school, and its potential to create ever more opportunities to develop social and global mobility, and if this is constantly reinforced with the staff themselves, then this will help them to frame their role within a wider context as well as the more immediate task-driven daily context with which they are most familiar. Sometimes, just seeing what we do in a slightly different light can make a huge difference to our motivation and what, therefore, we can achieve.

- Include them in the training and awareness sessions you are running for teaching staff, to introduce them to the concept of social and global mobility and to start them thinking about how they can personally and collectively make a difference.

Ideas for involving non-teaching staff in practical action and/or skills development

- See the section on teachers for related ideas.
- As with teachers, make it an expectation that all non-teaching

staff have a responsibility to help to promote the school's vision of greater social and global mobility. Your powers of influence and engagement will be called upon here, as there is a danger that this could appear to non-teaching staff as an added (unpaid) burden, whereas what you really want to achieve is a shift in emphasis, so that whatever roles or tasks staff are engaged with in school take on a slightly different, richer, hue.

- Of course, the more staff you can involve in practical action too, the more cohesive the school's vision can become, and the stronger its impact can be. Ask for their help to:
  - spread the message in the wider community about the school's vision and the practical activities that are going on in school.
  - encourage people from the wider community to come into school and sign up as volunteers, to contribute to the programmes that the school has already developed, and will develop further.
- Remind them of the powerful effect of their words and actions on young people. Simply by encouraging or praising, they can make a big difference.

If the school is proactive in developing opportunities for other adults to learn and develop themselves (including language skills courses), then non-teaching staff – like teachers and any other adults in the local community – can benefit from these too. It is in the interest of schools to keep investing in the learning of all its staff, so that the school community really is a learning community. As they learn and acquire new skills, non-teaching staff will acquire an ever greater capacity to become more socially and globally mobile too, and this will strengthen the vision of the school still further.

School boards (Sphere 2: the school community)

What is the school already doing to raise the awareness of the school board about social and global mobility?	What is the school already doing to involve the school board in practical action and/or skills development?
What does or should motivate the school board to get more involved in developing the school's vision of social and global mobility?	What can the school board contribute to the vision of developing social and global mobility?
How is the school engaging with the school board (eg through personal relationships, professional relationships, through influence, through outreach, and/or through a network)?	To what extent is the school really engaged with the school board? How could the school become better engaged with the school board?

How can we find out more about the school board's involvement with the school's vision for social and global mobility?

It is very important that the school board understands exactly why the school is focusing part of its activity on social and global mobility; after all, the school board is ultimately responsible for the vision and the strategic direction of the school. The relationship between school leaders and the school board or school governors should be close enough for strategic issues to be debated openly and honestly, and this should make it possible to sound out the members of the board both individually and collectively about what they believe about social and global mobility. All board members have a life beyond school, in different networks, and it will be very useful for the leadership team to discover how the members of the board perceive social and global mobility in the wider world, and to analyse what they think it would be useful for the school to do in order to prepare young people more effectively to be able to be mobile in the world. While you will want to place all of this within a wider context of the research you have gathered about best practice elsewhere, so that your strategy development is not just based on the ideas of the board and/or anecdotal evidence about the current workplace, it is nonetheless useful to explore the issue with board members and to elicit their ideas and insights. This will help you understand where your particularly sympathetic allies on the board might be, and how much work you will have to do in order to explain the rationale behind your proposals for action and change.

Ideas for raising the school board's awareness about social and global mobility

- Share with the board at an early stage your detailed thinking, the research you have gathered and your overall proposed strategy about strengthening the capacity of the school to develop social and global mobility.
- Invite the board to sessions you run in school for staff about the value of social and global mobility.
- Consider setting up a board sub-committee, made up of a mixture of board members and school staff members, to focus on social and global mobility. The brief of this sub-committee could cover any or all of the following:
  - Strategy development
  - Research
  - Monitoring and evaluating progress

Ideas for involving the school board in practical action and/or skills development

- Identify additional resources that will be useful for you – additional staff, perhaps, or additional time and/or skills such as the development of a social media strategy – and make a case with the board for the allocation of funds for these resources, in as much as it is within their power to make these funding decisions.
- If the members of the board are not already involved as volunteers in the school's work experience or mentoring programmes, then

enrol them. If they can give, for example, an hour of their time once a month to help students in the school understand more about the working world, and/or build their confidence to be able to live, work and move within it, then this will enhance the school's impact in social and global mobility.

- Involve the board in creating a strategy for influencing wider networks of people about the importance of social and global mobility. Challenge them to think about their own networks, how they can reach them and influence them. Discuss with them what this might look like in practice, what the practical outcomes of this influencing might be, and how they might benefit the school. Board members will also fall into other categories of stakeholders – local businesses, for example, or local government, or parents *etc*. What they bring additionally to these stakeholder groups is their greater knowledge of, and involvement in, the strategic development of the school. This position of privileged information and engagement means that it is reasonable to expect that they have an obligation to take a leading role both in helping to shape the awareness of these stakeholder groups about social and global mobility, and also in encouraging these stakeholder groups to become more actively involved.

Parents and immediate carers (Sphere 2: the school community)

What is the school already doing to raise the awareness of parents and immediate carers about social and global mobility?	What is the school already doing to involve parents and immediate carers in practical action and/or skills development?
What does or should motivate parents and immediate carers to get more involved in developing the school's vision of social and global mobility?	What can parents and immediate carers contribute to the vision of developing social and global mobility?
How is the school engaging with parents and immediate carers (eg through personal relationships, professional relationships, through influence, through outreach, and/or through a network)?	To what extent is the school really engaged with parents and immediate carers? How could the school become better engaged with parents and immediate carers?

How can we find out more about parents' and carers' involvement with the school's vision for social and global mobility?

If you have a parent council or parent association, ask them. Use an opportunity at a scheduled meeting to present your vision, focusing on the benefits for the current students – their children – and explaining how everything that the students do in school in fact in some way prepares them to be more socially and globally mobile. Parents – any stakeholders, in fact – need to understand first what is being presented to them before they can contribute effectively; once they do, and once they feel empowered to contribute to the school's vision with practical support, then many more creative ideas may emerge from this group.

Sometimes schools fear empowering parents, because of awkward experiences in the past, when parents have favoured their own children in activities, but if a school draws up a strong set of guidelines (a code of conduct) around expectations of volunteers, this helps. If it is also obvious that other stakeholder groups are being systematically drawn into the school to contribute to the work of the school, then this makes it easier for parents and carers to appreciate that while they are needed to contribute as parents to the development of their own child, they are being asked in this wider context to contribute their work and life experiences more generally, to more children.

Ideas for raising parents' and carers' awareness about social and global mobility

- Work with the parent council to identify how best to communicate messages to parents about the school's vision for social and global mobility sensitively, accurately and effectively. At the right moments, and in the most appropriate formats – and this is always going to be a hard judgement call – seek to inform parents about what you are trying to do to develop opportunities for greater social and global mobility. Remember to emphasise the forward-facing focus of this strategy – it is not about where families have come from, but where the students can all, equally, go to.

- Ask parents to think about who they know – through work or their other networks – who can help the school pursue this goal of social and global mobility.

- Keep inviting parents into school – the more familiar that parents are with the school, and the more they see the messages about developing social and global mobility around them and their children in school, the more the vision will make sense to them, and the more easily they will be able to communicate it to others.

Ideas for involving parents and carers in practical action and/or skills development

- Ask for parent volunteers to run extra-curricular clubs and activities. Most schools have at least some parents who do this already, and the advantage they bring is (for non-working parents or carers, at least) that they are often able to contribute to activities in and around school hours. Bringing areas of expertise into school which are not already present means that schools can extend students' opportunities and skills, and this directly contributes to their capacity for social and global mobility.

- Ask parents to contribute actively to one or more of the school's programmes or strategies in the areas of personal development, careers and/or culture (see The Individual Student section in this chapter for a comprehensive list). Work out what your guidelines are about parents working with their own children, and how you will manage communication and parental expectations. When parents contribute to school activities, they have to come to a point where they realise that although they are being asked to contribute because of their close interest in the school, and although they have ideas and perspectives to offer, from which the school could definitely benefit in some way, there will be (many) times when they are needed to be part of a team, directed by professionals at the school who are much more practised than they are in managing children.

- Ask parents to spread the word about what the school is doing, and encourage other adults in their workplace (or community groups, general networks *etc*) to become involved in the school's programmes which require volunteers (*eg* work experience, mentoring, personal development *etc*). The same can be asked of parents with regard to any other group to which they belong – community group, church, club *etc*.

As the school expands its range of opportunities to adults as well as to students, parents may find that opportunities arise for their own learning – more courses run on site, for example, or more access to digital courses through the school's online portal – and this inevitably has the potential to increase their personal capacity to become more socially and globally mobile. When schools pursue the Powerful Schools Vision, they can have a significant and positive impact on numerous stakeholder groups.

Volunteers in school (Sphere 2: the school community)

What is the school already doing to raise the awareness of volunteers about social and global mobility?	What is the school already doing to involve volunteers in practical action and/or skills development?
What does or should motivate volunteers to get more involved in developing the school's vision of social and global mobility?	What can volunteers contribute to the vision of developing social and global mobility?
How is the school engaging with volunteers (eg through personal relationships, professional relationships, through influence, through outreach, and/or through a network)?	To what extent is the school really engaged with volunteers? How could the school become better engaged with volunteers?

How can we find out more about volunteers' involvement with the school's vision for social and global mobility?

Schools often don't have a centralised list of all the volunteers that come into school, although they should already have policies and guidelines for managing volunteers (a legal requirement in most jurisdictions). A useful first step is therefore to gather together information about all the volunteers in school, whether or not they volunteer regularly or very occasionally. Many of the volunteers in school will fall into one of the other stakeholder groups, and it might make sense to allocate them in due course to these groups rather than a separate 'volunteer' group, largely for reasons of managing them efficiently – if the school is successful in engaging its multiple stakeholder groups, then the number of volunteers contributing to the activity of the school could become very large indeed, and may need to be subdivided by stakeholder group. This, however, is up to the school to decide – they may prefer to create a single pool of 'volunteers', among whom are people who are contributing to the school in a number of different ways.

Existing volunteers likely belong to one or more of the following stakeholder groups:

- School boards
- Parents and carers
- Wider families
- Community groups
- Local businesses
- People of local or national or international influence
- Other adults who live locally
- National businesses
- National organisations

If you decide to manage volunteers within each of the stakeholder groups, but you have any volunteers in school who do not fit into these stakeholder groups, you could either create a new appropriately named category for them, or treat them as 'other volunteers'. In any case, to find out to what extent they already believe in, are engaged with, and contribute to, the school's vision for social and global mobility, the best approach, after identifying who they are, is simply to get to know them and ask them directly, in whichever way works best for you as a school.

Ideas for raising volunteers' awareness about social and global mobility

- See the relevant section of this chapter for volunteers from each stakeholder group.
- Consider arranging a half day 'volunteers' conference or series of seminars to explain the thinking behind what you are seeking to achieve in school, and how they can contribute to this. This format lends itself as much to recruiting new volunteers as it does to educating current volunteers. When you have tweaked the structure of this event, and you have tracked its effectiveness in engaging and recruiting volunteers, this is potentially one of

the many structures that you can export and share with other schools (see the relevant section later in this chapter).

Ideas for involving volunteers in practical action and/or skills development

- See the relevant section of this chapter for volunteers from each stakeholder group.
- Volunteers can be used in practically every aspect of school activity – they just need to be managed according to the legal parameters within which you work. Ask the teaching and non-teaching staff to brainstorm how they would use volunteers in their area of school and come up with a list of opportunities.

It may be important to reassure staff that volunteers will never replace core staff, and it is certainly important to recognise that managing volunteers takes some resources, not least in planning how to keep children safe, as well as in working out how to make best use of the talents of the volunteers. Stress, however, that by bringing volunteers into school, the capacity of the school for demonstrable action will increase, and the school will be in a better position to make progress in re-orientating society's perceptions of schools. Ultimately, this can and should bring better funding and resourcing to schools – and volunteers can help make this happen.

Like parents, teachers and other adults, volunteers will also be able to benefit personally from the school's increasing range of opportunities aimed at adults as well as to students. A school focus on social and global mobility has the potential to be positive for everyone.

Wider families, including grandparents (Sphere 3: the local community)

What is the school already doing to raise the awareness of wider families about social and global mobility?	What is the school already doing to involve wider families in practical action and/or skills development?
What does or should motivate wider families to get more involved in developing the school's vision of social and global mobility?	What can wider families contribute to the vision of developing social and global mobility?
How is the school engaging with wider families (eg through personal relationships, professional relationships, through influence, through outreach, and/or through a network)?	To what extent is the school really engaged with wider families? How could the school become better engaged with wider families?

How can we find out more about the involvement of wider families with the school's vision for social and global mobility?

Ask the students to ask them. A note of caution here: because of the complexity of families, it is important to think carefully about how to explore the family connections of the students in school. A laser-like focus is needed on the purpose of this reflection, if it is not to falter on the grounds of ethical and safeguarding concerns. These need to be considered carefully, and it is much easier to do this when the aim of this activity is focused. Be very clear in reaching out to families through the students: you want to establish more clearly who students are connected to, in order to help them as well as you understand who they are, and to start exploring the potential power of these family connections in contributing to school and in influencing the world.

A guiding ethical principle in this task is transparency – students need to know exactly what you are doing. Another guiding principle is respect for individual circumstances – few families are without their internal traumas and complex relationships, and these will need to be explored carefully. Ultimately, the welfare of the child who is the student at school is paramount, and this overrides any desire to connect with their family members far and wide. This said, unless you gather information about families, you will not know where to tread carefully. The easiest way, of course, is not to gather any information at all, but this is self-defeating if a school is striving to become powerful in effecting change – knowledge contributes to power.

When you are comfortable with your ethical position on reaching out to wider families via the students themselves, you could capture the information you gather about these networks pictorially or in any suitable format. At some point in most school curricula, time is devoted to teaching students how to construct a family tree (and setting them the research task of finding out who is in their family tree) – this activity can be extended in a number of ways, so as to contribute to the school's (and the student's) understanding of who families are and how they connect. If students can be empowered to look at how their families have become more socially or globally mobile, and to focus on this rather than their relative social standing compared to one another, then this makes mobility (and potential for greater mobility) the platform for discussion, rather than how socio-economically successful families are, and/or how many foreign holidays they take. A central principle of this book is that each young person can have an equal chance for social and global mobility – it is up to the school, however, to drive the creation of opportunities that put this principle into practice.

Ideas for raising the awareness of wider families about social and global mobility

- When students research their family trees, it is an opportunity for them to discuss with wider family members what is meant by social mobility and how these connections can help communication and understanding. This kind of discussion – while potentially sensitive, and one which must be handled extremely well – is a key means of raising the awareness of wider families about social and global mobility. Students may need help in framing the language around the task, however, and in communicating its purpose, so the school may decide that it is best to give a written explanatory note – and, if deemed appropriate, to make participation optional.

- Bring families into school and communicate with them while they are there. A number of schools, for example, run 'Grandparents' Days', which are very much like Open Days, but in which grandparents are made to feel particularly special. The reasons why schools do not run such days fall usually into the following categories:

  - The amount of time and effort it takes to organise such days.

  - The disruption to everyday school activity.

  - Sensitivity to family circumstances – students who may not have grandparents, for instance, or who may have suffered recent bereavement, or who are estranged from their grandparents, or whose families are fractured (meaning, perhaps, that grandparents of the same student may themselves be in conflict).

  - Lack of clarity about the purpose of a themed day like this.

Addressing the last point first is perhaps the best way to progress: within the overarching goal of developing schools to become powerful places of social change, families are essential, and it is important for the school to engage with them, both to help them understand what is going on in school and to help them see what they need to do to further the aims of the school. If this purpose is clear, the time and effort required become worth it, and 'disruption' is reconfigured as 'activity'. It is all a matter of perspective and vision.

The issue of sensitivity to family circumstances is trickier, in part because most schools do not have the detailed information which might help guide them in this area (even if they have successfully implemented information-gathering activities such as family trees). Besides, it is highly likely that in any school, at any given point, there will be some significant sensitivities which schools will need to take into account. This does not mean, however, that days such as these should not happen – it simply means that they need to be constructed carefully. Schools can choose to do this in a number of ways, including communicating separately with families with particular needs, to explain, sensitively, why the day has been put on. Safer and easier, perhaps, is to make the day more inclusive, aiming it at 'family members near or far and wide, carers, and all those who have a particular family interest in what goes on in this school'. Some of the power to invite needs to lie with the students themselves; they can be encouraged to spread the word.

Make sure that the aim of the day is clear. The displays of student work may be great, but for the day to be effective in meeting an aim of communicating about social and global mobility, and of highlighting their pivotal social role, schools need also to reveal their workings to their audience. This can be done in a number of ways:

- Explicit communication about the purpose of the day – to show families what it is all for.
- Clear vision and mission statements, prominently displayed, highlighting the social and global purpose of the day.
- Explicit reflection on how important schools are in society. As we saw earlier in this book, this understanding can no longer be taken for granted, and has to be emphasised at every opportunity.

Ideas for involving wider families in practical action and/or skills development

- In order to capitalise on occasions when wider families are in school, the school needs not only to make its visitors aware of the school's role in developing social and global mobility, and to inspire them to think that they can be involved, but it also needs to capture the willingness of the audience to engage in the wider purpose of schools. This can also be done in a number of ways:
  - Encourage visitors to sign up to receive further information through the website and social media platforms.
  - Encourage them to volunteer on one of the school's programmes – work experience, mentoring, personal development *etc.*

- Encourage them to commit to time – perhaps even just an hour of their time, once a month – and give them examples of how they could use this hour, either inside or outside school, to help students and/or the school, and/or schools in general, in their pursuit of the aims of the Powerful Schools Vision.

As the school expands its range of opportunities to adults as well as to students, wider families – like parents, teachers and other adults more generally – are likely to find that opportunities arise for their own learning – more courses run on the school site, for example, or more access to digital courses through the school's online portal – and this inevitably has the potential to increase their personal capacity to become more socially and globally mobile. When schools pursue the Powerful Schools Vision, they can have a significant and positive impact on numerous stakeholder groups.

Former students (Sphere 3: the local community)

What is the school already doing to raise the awareness of former students about social and global mobility?	What is the school already doing to involve former students in practical action and/or skills development?
What does or should motivate former students to get more involved in developing the school's vision of social and global mobility?	What can former students contribute to the vision of developing social and global mobility?
How is the school engaging with former students (eg through personal relationships, professional relationships, through influence, through outreach, and/or through a network)?	To what extent is the school really engaged with former students? How could the school become better engaged with former students?

How can we find out more about the involvement of former students with the school's vision for social and global mobility?

Schools which prepare their students from their arrival in school to consider that they will in time be former students, and will have a responsibility to give back to the school community in some way, and then keep in touch with these students once they have left and continue to value them, are generally going to have a much better strike rate in involving former students in the future. Moreover, continuing to keep in touch with former students during the years immediately after they leave school is another essential prerequisite for success in involving former students in the work of the school at a later stage. Although the early post-school years are a time when students often move around a lot, and when their attention is focused forward, not backward on school, and although this is a time when they are still growing up, and are naturally still self-centred, it is really important for the school to maintain positive ties with them, so that they retain a sense of belonging to the school. The real value of former students of course usually lies later, when they have learned about the world and have carved their own way; at this point in their lives, they are then in a position to communicate back to current students what they have learned, and can also, importantly, help with pathways and opportunities for these students, all from the perspective of someone who has been through the same school that they are attending now, and who therefore has something deeply in common with them.

All of this suggests that if your school does not have a Former Students' Association with whom you can communicate and which you can use to help you, you should create one by bringing on board a few active and sympathetic former students and setting them the task of establishing an Association which is inclusive, connects with former students, and will, amongst other elements, enable the school to communicate directly with former students and seek their involvement in the work of the school on social and global mobility. If a Former Students' Association already exists, engage with it and use it. Work out carefully who will be responsible for managing this relationship in school, and how to gain maximum benefit from the relationship through focused activity. Former Students' Associations often have a history and a specifically social element – this is fine, and to be supported, but it is not the focus of the Powerful Schools Vision, and schools should beware of diluting their own focus and activity by becoming overly engaged in supporting the activity of their FSA. Many schools use their FSA for fundraising – again, this is commendable and almost certainly to be supported, but it is different from the awareness-raising and engagement of the Powerful Schools Vision, and will require a different kind of approach and a different contact with the school. For awareness-raising and engagement in action to be effective, it needs to be targeted and not dissipated through involvement in all the other aspects of the activity of a Former Students' Association.

A final word about Former Students' Associations – it makes enormous sense for communication with former students to be handled by committees of active former students, especially if they are committed to openness and inclusivity, and getting as many former students connected as possible. However, not all former students come from the same mould, or have had the same experience of school (far from it), or will even want to be defined as former students, and schools must remain open-minded as to how they communicate with, and engage, all the students who have previously been to the school. The prime focus is on reaching out to as many people as possible to get them involved in the development of social and global mobility, and schools will need to be mindful of this.

Ideas for raising the awareness of former students about social and global mobility

- Build a strong relationship with your Former Students' Association and use any newsletters they produce, and/or their social media platform (and don't rule out perhaps using the occasion of any social reunions they might organise), to communicate what the school is doing to promote social and global mobility.

- Encourage former students to continue to follow the school on its own social media platforms, so that they remain connected and can see what is happening in school to develop social and global mobility.

- In communications with the school community, regularly include stories about what former students are doing in life. Each person will have a unique story, and there will be an enormous variety across the range of former students, not least because of the age range of the former students – from 18 to 100, potentially, depending on the age of the school. By telling these stories – and including the 'downs' as well as the 'ups' – the school can build a greater awareness in current students of the different paths that people can take in life, and what happens when they grasp opportunities. These stories will soon percolate into the former student community: the subjects of the stories will share them, as will people who knew them, and there is a chance that they will then remain connected in order to read the next story. Former students, then, as well as current students, are able to appreciate what social and global mobility can really mean in practice, especially if this is explicitly referred to in the story.

- Encourage the development of work-focused networks of former students, *ie* opportunities for former students to connect with other former students who work in the same field. From a participant's perspective, these networks can be really helpful in building relationships and finding opportunities; from the school's perspective, they are particularly useful because they provide a source of people who are (hopefully) increasingly connected with the school and its vision, and so are more likely to be willing to become involved in practical action and/or developing the skills of current students.

Ideas for involving former students in practical action and/or skills development

- Ask them to come back to school and volunteer for the school's programmes, including mentoring current students.
- If they are able to offer work experience placements to students in their own workplace, ask them to sign up to do so.
- Seek out former students who have spent time abroad, either travelling or working, and ask them to come back to school to share their experiences, and to explain how they went about organising this part of their life, and what they learned about other cultures and customs.
- Encourage all former students to use their networks to spread the word about what their old school is doing to promote social and global mobility, and what schools can do in general.

Former students too can benefit from any increase which the school makes in the courses and opportunities it opens to the community more generally – more courses run on site, for example, or more access to digital courses through the school's online portal. Participation in these courses and these opportunities has the potential to increase the personal capacity of former students to become more socially and globally mobile. They will gain as well as give.

Above all, try to gather as much information as possible about your former students, and track them as they move through their careers and lives. You want to be able to draw on them, to support them and to work out how effective the school has been in supporting their social and global mobility; you are going to need to keep as much evidence as you can about them.

Community groups, including charities, clubs and voluntary groups (Sphere 3: the local community)

What is the school already doing to raise the awareness of community groups about social and global mobility?	What is the school already doing to involve community groups in practical action and/or skills development?
What does or should motivate community groups to get more involved in developing the school's vision of social and global mobility?	What can community groups contribute to the vision of developing social and global mobility?
How is the school engaging with community groups (eg through personal relationships, professional relationships, through influence, through outreach, and/or through a network)?	To what extent is the school really engaged with community groups? How could the school become better engaged with community groups?

How can we find out more about the involvement of community groups with the school's vision for social and global mobility?

Many staff and parents will be active members of local community groups, and an initial audit (and subsequent audits with the relevant stakeholder groups) should help to identify where some of these close links are. It is also worth tasking a member of staff to draw up as comprehensive a list as possible of all the local community groups that they can think of, identifying:

- what they believe in / stand for / do.
- why they might be interested in contributing to a Vision of Powerful Schools which helps develop social and global mobility.

Some of these groups will work with young people – in many cases the same young people who are students at the school – and other groups will focus on different demographics. Each will have its own, usually quite specific, area of interest, and it will be up to the school to decide which of these are worth approaching first, and with what aim in mind. Schools have nothing to lose by simply asking the question of how these groups think that they might be able to contribute to the school's vision of developing social and global mobility, and how they think they might benefit from it. Some very interesting synergies might emerge from such conversations, and the relationships which grow out of them could prove mutually fruitful.

Ideas for raising the awareness of community groups about social and global mobility

- Meet with local youth groups and other community groups which work directly with the same young people who attend your school (eg sports clubs, theatre groups, Guides/Scouts, youth clubs, after school clubs *etc*). These groups are contributing significantly to the personal development of your students. Explain what you are doing and why you have a focus on social and global mobility; see what synergies emerge. As part of your drive to understand as much about your students as possible, it is in any case extremely worthwhile developing close links with these groups as it enables all parties involved to have a better and more rounded understanding of the individual young people and the different parts of their lives.

- Invite other community groups into school to see what you are doing. Some schools successfully run annual community fairs, where they host a mini-convention or a series of presentations by a number of different community groups. As well as enabling the school to develop its relationships with these groups, it also helps community groups to connect with one another, and the fact that this is happening in school sends a strong message about the school as an enabler and connector – a hub of activity. In developing the concept of a community fair, schools may have been motivated initially by a number of different reasons, perhaps primarily focused on giving back to the local community, but it is only a small step from this position to recognising the value of these relationships in contributing to the vision of Powerful Schools as hubs of social and global mobility. Once schools have identified what they hope to gain from even stronger relationships with community groups (see ideas for action below), they need to be as transparent as possible with these groups in order to inspire and engage them.

- Focus some of the school's external communication – digitally and through the media – about what is happening in school to promote social and global mobility in places which local community groups will access. This might involve putting up notices on local community noticeboards, contributing articles to local church magazines, and/or communicating through the local media.

- Offer the school as a venue to local community groups for regular meetings. This brings them into the school and allows them to feel comfortable there, as well as to encounter the visible signs of the Powerful Schools Vision which will be very apparent once you have raised significant internal awareness of the strategy.

Ideas for involving community groups in practical action and/or skills development

- Community groups offer an excellent opportunity for students to carry out volunteer work and work experience; they should certainly be signed up to the school's work experience and community service programmes.

- People who lead or contribute to the work of community groups usually have significant and interesting practical experiences and skills which could enhance some of the school's other programmes aimed at developing social and global mobility, including careers awareness and personal development programmes, and they should be encouraged to get involved in these.

- Develop a rich 'local affairs' strand in the curriculum, drawing together all the topic or curriculum areas throughout the school that relates to the local community, and map this against what you have found out about the interests and motivations of local community groups. Identify gaps, and opportunities for local community groups to fill these gaps; invite them into school to give a real and visible focus for learning in these areas.

- People involved in community groups often have very interesting lives. Invite them in to speak to the students in relevant clubs and societies, and as part of a lecture series.

Local businesses – small, medium and large (Sphere 3: the local community)

What is the school already doing to raise the awareness of local businesses about social and global mobility?	What is the school already doing to involve local businesses in practical action and/or skills development?
What does or should motivate local businesses to get more involved in developing the school's vision of social and global mobility?	What can local businesses contribute to the vision of developing social and global mobility?
How is the school engaging with local businesses (eg through personal relationships, professional relationships, through influence, through outreach, and/or through a network)?	To what extent is the school really engaged with local businesses? How could the school become better engaged with local businesses?

How can we find out more about the involvement of local businesses with the school's vision for social and global mobility?

The internal audit will be an initial source of evidence in finding out how the school already interacts with local businesses. Many schools have multiple and well-developed relationships with local businesses, and engage with this stakeholder group very well indeed. There is always scope for more activity, however. In order to explore what this might look like, you also need to find out more about local businesses themselves, as a precursor to thinking about how you could involve them more. Start by defining what you mean by local – what kind of geographical area, for instance – and then ask yourselves these questions about local businesses:

- How many are there?
- Who are they?

- What do they do?
- What is their reach?
- Are they grouped in networks?
- How are some of our more immediate stakeholders in the school community (*eg* teachers and parents) connected with these businesses?
- Are we aware of any particular interests that local businesses already have in developing social and global mobility?

The answers to these questions will help paint a picture of local businesses and will start to suggest and prompt specific ideas for engaging them in the Powerful Schools Vision.

At this point it is also a good idea to research all the available 'work skills' or 'life skills' programmes available to young people. Several banks run sponsored programmes, and some of the larger companies do too. Other programmes such as The Duke of Edinburgh's Award have been around for many years and are very established. Programmes such as the Model United Nations or English Speaking Union debating competitions develop skills which are extremely useful for developing confidence in the workplace, and technology-focused competitions and initiatives (*eg* the Lego League or the Hour of Code) develop teamwork and collaborative skills as well as some of the essential technology skills that young people need if they are to have the widest range of opportunities later on in life. Some of these programmes will already be embedded in the work of local youth groups (see section on community groups) and carried out very successfully by them; others may be run in school already. A school cannot run every programme going, but with a committed large group of active local businesspeople, the school can offer much, much more beyond the curriculum. These programmes have the added advantage of providing a ready-made structure, so that the school does not need to design it from scratch. In time, schools will want to personalise and probably develop all of their programmes, because they need them to respond to the practical requirements of their specific students, and because the school's thinking will evolve significantly, but adapting programmes into which other people have put a significant amount of work, including preparing useful materials, is a good start –

and the frameworks that these programmes offer make it easier for local businesses to see at a glance how they can help.

Ideas for raising the awareness of local businesses about social and global mobility

- Invite them into school. Organise a seminar or series of seminars to introduce local businesses to what social and global mobility is all about, and ask for their help in some of the existing and new programmes that the school wants to offer to young people.

- Focus some of the school's external communication – digitally and through the media – about what is happening in school to promote social and global mobility on places which local businesses will access. This might involve preparing short articles for local business magazines or the local newspaper, or even putting up notices on local community noticeboards (physical or digital). Research which newsfeeds and online sources of local news are popular amongst local businesses and make sure that the school is connected to them and generates content for them – short snippets of information about what is going on in school, details of events *etc.*

- Target networks of local businesses – ask to speak at some of their local forums, and become part of the groups. Remember that a school is a local business too, and a significant contributor to the local economy, not least in the number of staff that it employs. School leaders are business leaders too – with a particularly strong socially motivated vision and drive to engage other business leaders in the school's work, in order to enhance the overall impact that the school can have.

Ideas for involving local businesses in practical action and/or skills development

- Sign them up to the school's work experience programme, so that students can spend a week or two at least in Year 10 or Year 11, usually, in a local work environment. The more businesses you can sign up, the more opportunities the students will have. Involve the local businesses in helping to design the structure of the week, and the kind of tasks that the students should experience – and report back on – during this spell in the workplace.

- Arrange a programme of regular visits to the school by people working in local business, so that they can talk to students of all ages about what they do. The more of these visits you can arrange, the more integrated they will become into the daily life of the school, the greater the number of students who will have access to them, and the smaller the groups of students meeting with each visitor can be. People are often put off coming into school because they are nervous about addressing and managing large groups of potentially highly inquisitive children who have not yet always learned how to mask feelings such as indifference and boredom; make it easier for them by preparing them and by making the groups smaller (while ensuring that all students can benefit – no-one can be excluded).

- Arrange regular reciprocal visits to workplaces by students of all ages, so that they can see and become familiar with working environments. Prepare for these ahead of time, and follow them up in school afterwards with detailed reflections, in order to cement the learning from them. Remember – the more familiar students are, and the more aware they are, of all the opportunities available to them later in life, the more confident they will be to make choices that stretch them.

- If you don't already have a work-shadowing programme, design one (in conjunction with local businesses). This differs from work experience in that it involves students in a much greater focus on observation than on actual tasks, and is particularly appropriate for introducing students to higher level areas of work, including management, finance, legal work, advertising *etc.* A successful work-shadowing programme will have:

  - a clear set of goals and expectations.

  - set tasks and expected outcomes, *eg* questions that students must answer about their experiences, a guided reflection log, and a presentation that they must give after the event on certain aspects of what they have discovered.

  - time for the business mentor to discuss with the students

what they have seen, in order to answer their further questions and to help them to process their experience.

- variety – which could be within a single business or across a number of businesses. This latter structure is particularly appropriate for themed work-shadowing programmes, so that a single student can see how *eg* marketing is treated in different ways in 4 or 5 different companies, over the course of, say, a week.

- Together with the local businesses, design or develop your in-school 'work readiness' programme, and involve people from local businesses in it as speakers, mentors and supervisors (and assessors, if you make it a formal course). This programme could include elements such as CV writing, interview skills, how to dress and present yourself, the etiquette of business life *etc*, and is effectively a training course for the workplace.

- Work with the local businesses to design extended work experience and/or work shadowing programmes, perhaps in school holidays, where students can have the opportunity to apply to work in local businesses for two or three weeks, or on a regular basis. This programme could build on the 'work readiness' programmes run in school, so that students are to some extent trained in school for the role they will be fulfilling.

- Set up a comprehensive mentoring programme for students throughout the school, to introduce them to life in local business. Students could be grouped into small numbers and meet regularly with their mentor to discuss issues that affect working life, *eg* money, the regulations that businesses have to follow, marketing and brand development, managing staff *etc*.

- Consider designing similar programmes for former students, as part of your strategy also to engage former students (see the section on Former students). Former students – young and old – may not have had the same opportunities as current students, and may also be at a stage in their lives where they want or need to change direction. Several organisations offer courses and programmes to support people who want to get into work or want to return to the workplace after a break, and you will certainly not want to compete with these, but the knowledge which you develop in designing and testing robust, effective work experience, work-shadowing and mentoring programmes will be extremely valuable, and will also be transferable. Think creatively about how you can enable and co-ordinate the engagement of local businesses in helping other sectors of society than just current students.

Local people of influence (Sphere 3: the local community)

What is the school already doing to raise the awareness of local people of influence about social and global mobility?	What is the school already doing to involve local people of influence in practical action and/or skills development?
What does or should motivate local people of influence to get more involved in developing the school's vision of social and global mobility?	What can local people of influence contribute to the vision of developing social and global mobility?
How is the school engaging with local people of influence (eg through personal relationships, professional relationships, through influence, through outreach, and/or through a network)?	To what extent is the school really engaged with local people of influence? How could the school become better engaged with local people of influence?

How can we find out more about the involvement of local people of influence with the school's vision for social and global mobility?

You may decide, on reflection, to reject this particular grouping and instead to absorb all locally-based people who have any influence under another relevant heading, for example:

- School boards
- Parents and carers
- Wider families
- Community groups
- Local businesses
- Other adults who live locally

They may even fall into the following categories:

- People of national or international influence
- National businesses
- National organisations

It does not always sit easily with schools – who have an essentially egalitarian approach to the world and who are seeking to prepare all their students to be equally socially and globally mobile – if they have to identify certain people within their networks as having potentially more external influence than others. After all, as explained in Chapter 5, every adult has the potential to exert influence in numerous ways, whether through informal conversations with friends to spreading the word throughout their networks or in more high profile ways such as communicating actively through social and more traditional media. Particularly now, as the age of authority diminishes and the power of peer review and trusted relationships increases, anyone can be a person of local influence if they set themselves up to be so. It is undeniable, however, that some people do actually have more influence than others – either more impact and/or more reach. This may be because of a position that they hold (eg local politician), or it may be because they are more active on social media and have a wide circle with whom they communicate. Schools are wise to recognise and acknowledge this, rather than to reject the notion of 'people of local influence' entirely out of hand. Instead, if they take time to identify who these people are, and seek to understand what motivates them, and where their interests may coincide with those of the school, then they may find these people a very useful conduit to help strengthen the school's activity and cement its position in the public psyche as a central hub for the development of social and global mobility.

Ideas for raising the awareness of local people of influence about social and global mobility

- See the relevant sections on other stakeholders for a range of ideas on how to raise the awareness of local people of influence.
- Invite them into school to see what is going on. Be explicit – you are seeking to build a relationship because you know that they are committed to the development of the local area, and of local

people, and so are you. You have the means and the vision to make a difference to the opportunities for young people (and others too) to experience greater social and global mobility, and you want them to help you so that you can work together to the same end.

Ideas for involving local people of influence in practical action and/or skills development

- See the relevant sections on other stakeholders for a range of ideas about how to involve local people of influence.
- Ask them to speak to the students about their own life experiences. The more exposure that students have to different perspectives and different stories, the more robust their understanding of the world and its varied opportunities can become.
- Ask for help in bringing more people into school – how can they help influence others to become involved in the school's vision?
- Ask for help in spreading the word about what is going on in school. Perhaps they might create opportunities for you to access other decision-makers (or members of other stakeholder groups which you have yet to access fully), in order to share what you are doing and ask for more help.

Local government and local education departments (Sphere 3: the local community)

What is the school already doing to raise the awareness of local government and local education departments about social and global mobility?	What is the school already doing to involve local government and local education departments in practical action and/or skills development?
What does or should motivate local government and local education departments to get more involved in developing the school's vision of social and global mobility?	What can local government and local education departments contribute to the vision of developing social and global mobility?
How is the school engaging with local government and local education departments (eg through personal relationships, professional relationships, through influence, through outreach, and/or through a network)?	To what extent is the school really engaged with local government and local education departments? How could the school become better engaged with local government and local education departments?

How can we find out more about the involvement of local government and local education departments with the school's vision for social and global mobility?

If you have good communication links with the local town, city or state government departments which oversee education in your school, then you will know what their policies are on how they think schools can develop social and global mobility. If these aren't clear, or can't easily be found in the official documentation, then ask for clarification, but the chances are that this is an area of social policy development which local government and local education departments are keen to promote, because of the potential impact on closing the attainment gap and ensuring access to equal future opportunities for all students. Do check that you are engaged with any and all of the local government programmes which are specifically focused on developing social and global mobility; not only is this kind of pre-prepared, pre-trialled programme often easier to implement than programmes which you have to invent from scratch, but your participation will strengthen your links with this particular stakeholder group.

Ideas for raising the awareness of local government and local education departments about social and global mobility

- If you think that your local government education department needs to focus more on strategies to develop social and global mobility, then tell them so. Approach your main contact at the department and make your case; offer to share good practice and ask for an opportunity to do this when it will have maximum effective reach to other schools.

Ideas for involving local government and local education departments in practical action and/or skills development

- Local government can often facilitate action through a distribution of funding and resources; don't be afraid to make a case for what you have identified that you need. Staff time is one of the most valuable resources you can use to push forward strategic development, and it is worth exploring how you can attract more of this to your school. Is there, for example, a way in which you can be allocated or seconded some central government administrative staff time in order to facilitate the set-up or extension of programmes which will connect schools and/or stakeholders more effectively? If you don't ask, you won't know.

- Local government is staffed with people who could very usefully be mentors or guides to young people; sign them up for your school programmes. Equally, the local government department is an excellent destination for a work experience placement. Local government interaction with schools should not be limited to policy development and the internal workings of schools; it is also a workplace from which students can learn.

- In a similar vein, explore carefully with the local education department what links they have with other departments both in the local area and further afield – perhaps even internationally. Each of these links in their network has the potential to develop into an opportunity for students and/or staff, and/or indeed other individuals connected with schools, to develop their skills, confidence and experience in the wider world, and therefore to grow more ready to become socially and globally mobile. All it needs is creative thought – and the determination to see ideas through.

Further education institutions (Sphere 3: the local community)

What is the school already doing to raise the awareness of further education institutions about social and global mobility?	What is the school already doing to involve further education institutions in practical action and/or skills development?
What does or should motivate further education institutions to get more involved in developing the school's vision of social and global mobility?	What can further education institutions contribute to the vision of developing social and global mobility?
How is the school engaging with further education institutions (eg through personal relationships, professional relationships, through influence, through outreach, and/or through a network)?	To what extent is the school really engaged with further education institutions? How could the school become better engaged with further education institutions?

How can we find out more about the involvement of further education institutions with the school's vision for social and global mobility?

Look closely at the strategic development plans of local further education institutions and make a note of what they are doing to support social and global mobility. Because further education institutions often have a wide remit in terms of age range, type of course and projected destinations of their students, and because they often have a more vocational focus than schools, this means that in many cases they have built very successful, long term partnerships with local employers, and have developed a wide range of opportunities for their students to engage in practical activities which will boost their capacity for social mobility (and potentially global mobility, although many further education institutions have yet to embrace this fully, their focus being largely on the local and perhaps national community).

Ideas for raising the awareness of further education institutions about social and global mobility

- See the section on universities for relevant and similar ideas.
- Build relationships with your local further education institution – go and talk to them, share openly what you are trying to achieve, and work out together how you can work together for mutual benefit. If there is a local or national government context for this discussion – *ie* if there are policies in place which recommend this kind of collaboration – then it makes it easier for the conversation to lead to action, but it still requires at least one of the partners to reach out and make it happen.

Ideas for involving further education institutions in practical action and/ or skills development

- See the section on universities for relevant and similar ideas.
- Connect key members of staff and aim to work jointly, sharing staff and resources, and combining networks, on any or all of the following school-based programmes:
  - Work experience for students.
  - Personal development programmes, including confidence-building and communication skills.
  - Skills development programmes, including language development and digital skills.
  - Vocational courses aimed at developing work-readiness.
- Create opportunities to bring more mature further education students into school to share their life experiences (and experiences of study) with younger students.
- Think together about how you can use your facilities to offer holiday and weekend courses, so that learning can continue at all times of the week and year.
- Consider co-developing specific 'work-readiness' or 'global-readiness' qualifications, based on your shared experience of what students need in order to become effective global citizens. These qualifications could sit at various different

levels, from certificate to diploma; you could in due course seek accreditation within a number of assessment frameworks, which would enable the qualification to be offered to a much wider circle of students.

Other adults who live locally (Sphere 3: the local community)

What is the school already doing to raise the awareness of other adults in the community about social and global mobility?	What is the school already doing to involve other adults in the community in practical action and/or skills development?
What does or should motivate other adults in the community to get more involved in developing the school's vision of social and global mobility?	What can other adults in the community contribute to the vision of developing social and global mobility?
How is the school engaging with other adults in the community (eg through personal relationships, professional relationships, through influence, through outreach, and/or through a network)?	To what extent is the school really engaged with other adults in the community? How could the school become better engaged with other adults in the community?

How can we find out more about the involvement of other adults with the school's vision for social and global mobility?

Theoretically, if the school's engagement with all its other stakeholders is excellent, then this is a group which should need minimal attention; most adults who live locally, after all, usually belong to one or more of the other stakeholder groups – local community groups, businesses, parents, wider family, former students *etc*. However, in practice it is worth reaching out additionally to adults who live locally, even if they do belong to some of these other groups: even if the communication channels to and within these groups are outstanding, and everyone involved with them is fully informed about what the school is doing (which is unlikely), and has received an explicit request to get involved, there is a high chance that people in these groups will still often not think that this applies to them, or that they have anything to offer the school. (They might also need to be persuaded and inspired about their social responsibility and why they should be getting involved in the work of schools.) The school therefore needs to approach them directly, as individual citizens, and show them that they are very much in demand. This stakeholder group is also, of course, a catchall group to cover local people who do not fall into other stakeholder groups. It will be a very, very varied group, with no obvious single approach to finding out about their interest and engagement in social and global mobility; as the school builds its relationships with them, however, this will emerge.

Ideas for raising the awareness of other adults about social and global mobility

- Use local media channels as part of the school's communication campaign. Think about where local people gather their local information, and use these means of communication. Local newspapers, local online forums, local coffee shops, local banks, local supermarkets, local shopping centres and local libraries: all of these are places where adults who live locally might notice and gather information about what is going on in their local area, and where they might be most open to reading or hearing about what is happening at the local school.

- Invite local adults to open days and events at the school. These do not have to be events specifically focused on what the school is doing to promote social and global mobility, but by inviting the local community into school with open arms, the school is making an explicitly positive statement about how it welcomes engagement with the local community, together with an implicit statement that the school is an appropriate central hub around which the local community can coalesce. Moreover, during such events, all visitors can be exposed more easily to information and evidence of what the school believes about its key role in leading the development of social and global mobility in society, and what it is actually doing about it.

Ideas for involving other adults in practical action and/or skills development

- Put out a 'call to arms' to get adults involved in school. Think about organising a campaign in conjunction with an organisation, such as the local education authority to bring adults into schools. As the first step in a drive to get more adults into schools as mentors preparing students for the workplace, for example, the local education department or a group of schools could publicise a 'come into school' day, in which local adults are invited to hear how they can get involved in school, spend some time with students (perhaps talking about their specific career experiences, or in any other activity deemed appropriate by the school), and are encouraged to commit a certain amount of time per month to the school. Adults could confirm attendance by signing up online with some of their details so that the school has time to work out how to manage them, and also knows something of what to expect. This is an activity that could equally be done by a single school, but when several schools take part, it has the potential to give the day a higher profile and a greater legitimacy.

This next point is obvious to schools, but do set up a working group in school to consider how to manage adults coming into school. In due course, they should fit into the school's volunteer programme, and can be inducted and undergo regulatory police checks, but initially they will be visitors, and need to be managed appropriately. It is better to set up a group to manage this than to rely on an individual, largely because it is likely that a policy of welcoming other adults into school will lead to many more visitors in school, and the systems need to be able to accommodate this, so as to benefit from their expertise and still keep children safe. The scale of the task may be daunting for an individual, who might react, for example, by imposing restrictions on the numbers of manageable visitors – an approach which would limit the speed at which the vision can develop. It will be a challenge to manage lots of extra adults, but it is crucial for schools to remain solutions-focused, and not to erect hurdles to the policy. Making it clear from the outset that adults will undergo a police and other reference checks is a good starting point, as is trying to accomplish as many of these checks as possible ahead of their involvement in school. Make this as normal and friendly a process as possible, however – sometimes, unwittingly, schools sacrifice warmth and welcome to efficiency and adherence to the policies. Guides for visitors, a code of conduct, a named member of staff to whom other adults can turn: all of these could fall within the remit of the working group set up to manage the introduction of other adults into school.

Once these adults are engaged with schools, then they have the potential to offer help in the same way as parents; the focus initially, however, will most likely have to be on reaching out to them in the first place. This is where PR strategies focused on the role of schools come into their own, because essentially the rhetoric around schools needs to change if adults who are not directly connected with schools (and even those who are) are enabled to see that they have a purpose and a role in schools, and, indeed, an obligation to become involved.

National Government (Sphere 4: the national community)

What is the school already doing to raise the awareness of national government about social and global mobility?	What is the school already doing to involve national government in practical action and/or skills development?
What does or should motivate national government to get more involved in developing the school's vision of social and global mobility?	What can national government contribute to the vision of developing social and global mobility?
How is the school engaging with national government (eg through personal relationships, professional relationships, through influence, through outreach, and/or through a network)?	To what extent is the school really engaged with national government? How could the school become better engaged with national government?

How can we find out more about the involvement of national government with the school's vision for social and global mobility?

Find out what policy development is happening within government around social and global mobility. Search for papers that have been published, and note who (or which think tank or government department) was involved in researching and writing them, because they may be useful allies for you in the future. See if you can track what happened to these papers: where were they debated? What was the reaction? Who was particularly interested in the ideas? Was anyone or any particular department tasked with turning some of the ideas and recommendations into action? Who is driving a vision for social and global mobility generally at national government level? Don't forget too to investigate closely the work of the national Department for Education as regards social and global mobility. It may be that this is in any case where the main thrust of the government's action is focused, but if not, there will certainly be people in this department who are working on projects and plans which will directly improve social mobility, and which will ensure that education today contributes to creating the global citizens of tomorrow.

Ideas for raising the awareness of national government about social and global mobility

- Make direct contact with people and government departments you have identified as driving a vision for social and global mobility. Go and talk to them about the Powerful Schools Vision, and tell them what you are doing.

- Offer to connect with other schools and to share with them the experience of piloting and running programmes for students, staff and others. Offer to speak at national conferences or seminars run by the government.

- Talk to your local MP or parliamentary representative. If you can interest her/him in what you are doing, you may have a strong ally.

- Find out what national bodies who represent teachers (*eg* teacher unions and professional associations) are doing to influence government policy about social and global mobility. They will often have the ear of national policy-makers – if you can talk with them and influence the direction of their thinking, then this will provide another way into national government, in order to give your ideas an airing.

Ideas for involving national government in practical action and/or skills development

- When you have built a relationship with sympathetic people in the national government, ask for their help and support. They can be great enablers, and if they put their backing behind you, they can connect you with other bodies who are working in similar areas, which strengthens the action you are able to take. They may also be able to provide you with access to sources of funding and extra staff support.

- Don't forget that any connections you make can directly benefit your students too, by providing them with access to another workplace. Negotiate arrangements to bring your students into national government offices – as visitors, as work experience students, and/or as interns. You could also create opportunities for your former students too, which has the added benefit of engaging this stakeholder group more effectively with the Powerful Schools Vision.

- Equally, by bringing civil servants and politicians into school, to meet students, to talk with them and – although this is less likely, given the constraints on their time and the number of schools and groups for whom they have responsibility – even to mentor them, you will be extending the knowledge, understanding and confidence of the students about what they can achieve in life, and this directly contributes to their social and global mobility. Make sure that you persuade politicians and civil servants to come into school regularly.

National businesses (Sphere 4: the national community)

What is the school already doing to raise the awareness of national businesses about social and global mobility?	What is the school already doing to involve national businesses in practical action and/or skills development?
What does or should motivate national businesses to get more involved in developing the school's vision of social and global mobility?	What can national businesses contribute to the vision of developing social and global mobility?
How is the school engaging with national businesses (eg through personal relationships, professional relationships, through influence, through outreach, and/or through a network)?	To what extent is the school really engaged with national businesses? How could the school become better engaged with national businesses?

How can we find out more about the involvement of national businesses with the school's vision for social and global mobility?

The internal audit will be a prime source of evidence in finding out how the school engages with national businesses, but there is more that can be done to identify potential key partners. Start by doing an online search for 'business' plus 'social mobility' and/or 'global mobility': this will enable you to start building up a good picture of which companies are really active in the field of developing social and global mobility, and what they are doing. This is information which you can use in a number of ways:

- to find out what projects these businesses are supporting – where, what and how.
- to develop, as a result of this, ideas about how you might work with them, to help further their goals as well as yours.
- to develop ideas about how you can draw on their experience

of working with schools or other educational institutions to develop partnerships with other companies.

Ideas for raising the awareness of national businesses about social and global mobility

- See the section on local businesses for ideas about how to raise the awareness of national businesses who have a geographically local base.

- Plan a strategy for getting your message out to businesses. You will need a solid and readily accessible information base on which to build – probably a section of your website dedicated to how you are working with employers and businesses, and what the benefits are for everyone involved. Case studies and examples would sit very well here. In addition, you need to decide which businesses you want to target, and how. The first step in engaging any business in action centred on your school will be to clarify exactly what social and global mobility are, why they are important, and what you believe you can do, together, to make them more of a reality for all the young people in your community. By now, if you have absorbed the messages outlined in the early chapters of this book, and have practised communicating them as you have discussed them within school and with other stakeholders, you will be confident in delivering the messages. All that remains, therefore, is to be bold – to know that you have a powerful message to communicate and that you are the best people to be leading this drive on behalf of the next generation.

Ideas for involving national businesses in practical action and/or skills development

- See the section on local businesses for ideas about how to involve national businesses who have a geographically local base. Many of these ideas will apply equally to businesses which do not have a local base, particularly if you make use of communications technology to connect people. Mentoring of students can be done via Skype; lectures and interactive talks can be delivered through webinars. Thinking creatively about how to connect people can make very effective use of time, and can maximise the opportunities that national businesses can offer.

- These opportunities can also include financial support, as most national businesses have funds which they dedicate specifically to social projects. Consider carefully how you might use additional funds if they were allocated to you, and take time to explore the criteria that your target businesses use to decide how to spend the money which they want to use for social projects. Can you come up with ideas for projects which will meet these criteria? These might potentially include contributing financially to the funding (including the staff costs) of programmes in school such as work experience, mentoring, international connections *etc.*

- Think about how your staff might benefit from links with national businesses, and vice-versa. Could you design a jointly-run professional development programme where teachers shadow business employees, and vice-versa? Perhaps you could look at secondment programmes, too. When teachers are stretched to see the world of work from a different perspective, this will feed back into their interactions with their students, and into the awareness-raising programmes you are running at school.

- Explore the increasing number of programmes designed and run by national businesses to support social change, focused on young people. A number of banks run financial awareness courses, for example, some power companies run environmental awareness programmes, and other organisations run life skills programmes and programmes to support *eg* girls into STEM subjects. Much is happening in the business world to support social and global mobility, and schools should be tapping into this.

- Large businesses may also allocate a proportion of their advertising/marketing budget to sponsorship. If you are planning an event that will bring together various different stakeholders, particularly if these are groups which the business wants to reach, consider pitching for sponsorship to cover costs, including the staffing costs necessary to organise and administer the event. You will need to be transparent with all your stakeholders about what the benefits are to the school as well as to the sponsor, but sponsorship is nonetheless a legitimate way to redirect funds generated in the wider society back into the vital work of schools.

- Work experience in businesses with a national focus can be eye-opening for young people, and can really build their awareness of, and confidence in, the national arena. Wherever possible, schools should try to build relationships with companies which will enable students to experience a different perspective on the world of work, ideally in a different city. If they can prove to themselves that they can fend for themselves, then they are well on the way to developing a robustness and 'can do' attitude that will underpin their own social and global mobility.

People of national influence (Sphere 4: the national community)

What is the school already doing to raise the awareness of people of national influence about social and global mobility?	What is the school already doing to involve people of national influence in practical action and/or skills development?
What does or should motivate people of national influence to get more involved in developing the school's vision of social and global mobility?	What can people of national influence contribute to the vision of developing social and global mobility?
How is the school engaging with people of national influence (eg through personal relationships, professional relationships, through influence, through outreach, and/or through a network)?	To what extent is the school really engaged with people of national influence? How could the school become better engaged with people of national influence?

How can we find out more about the involvement of people of national influence with the school's vision for social and global mobility?

You may or may not think you know anyone who has some kind of national influence – but given the connectedness of today's world, you will be closer than you realise. It is unlikely, of course, to be an early strategic priority for you to seek someone (or some people) who can help you promote your ideas on a national stage so that other schools and organisations can understand them and contribute to what you are doing. However, remember that increased external interest may bring useful support; and it can only be an advantage to find out who is in your wider school network and to work out what interests and motivates them, and how this might coincide with what you are aiming for in school. Keep an eye out as you discover more about your stakeholders, and don't be afraid to ask to be connected to people with national influence.

Ideas for raising the awareness of people of national influence about social and global mobility

- Just talk to them. Share your vision and show them practical examples of what you are doing, and what you have achieved so far. Perfect your 'elevator speech' – your 30 second summary of what you are doing and why, and what you want people to help you with. Ask them about their interests, and use this information to prompt creative thinking about what you might do together.

Ideas for involving people of national influence in practical action and/or skills development

- If people who are interested in what you are doing have the ability to be able to pass this information on to other people who might be able to support you, to become involved and to spread the word, this will be of enormous practical help to you.

- Depending on their personal and professional circumstances, these people might potentially contribute financially to the funding of programmes in school such as work experience, mentoring, international connections *etc.*

National organisations – charities/support groups/political groups/campaigning groups (Sphere 4: the national community)

What is the school already doing to raise the awareness of national organisations about social and global mobility?	What is the school already doing to involve national organisations in practical action and/or skills development?
What does or should motivate national organisations to get more involved in developing the school's vision of social and global mobility?	What can national organisations contribute to the vision of developing social and global mobility?
How is the school engaging with national organisations (eg through personal relationships, professional relationships, through influence, through outreach, and/or through a network)?	To what extent is the school really engaged with national organisations? How could the school become better engaged with national organisations?

How can we find out more about the involvement of national organisations with the school's vision for social and global mobility?

The first step in finding out how national organisations are involved in developing social and global mobility is to define what you mean by 'national organisation'. It is a very broad term – a catchall for structured and formalised activity which does not fall under the headings of 'business' or 'government'. A useful activity is to brainstorm names of organisations under a series of subheadings, either by type of group or by focus of group, for example:

- charities
- support groups

- religious groups
- political groups
- campaigning groups
- *etc*

or

- children and parents
- health
- business
- religion
- *etc*

Your initial audit will have revealed a number of existing relationships, and it will be up to you to determine whether these are sufficient for you for the time being. It is physically impractical to hope to develop individual relationships with every possible national organisation; what is perhaps more important is to ensure that the school has relationships with a range of different organisations, and that collectively these relationships offer access to a spread of sectors.

Some national organisations are very focused on social mobility (less so to date on global mobility), and already produce some excellent support materials, for example:

- the Sutton Trust in the UK – www.suttontrust.com – has conducted extensive research on social mobility and how to address this through education.
- the National Parent Forum of Scotland – www.npfs.org.uk – has a 'Careers in a Nutshell' pack which gives practical advice to young people and parents about developing work-readiness from an early age.

As part of your in-school strategy to explore what is cutting-edge in social and global mobility, a small group could usefully keep researching all of these materials, and keep a watching brief on documentation and examples of good practice. Only you know what is particularly relevant to your school situation, and this understanding will evolve as you pursue the goal of action leading towards greater social and global mobility.

Ideas for raising the awareness of national organisations about social and global mobility

- See the sections on national businesses and local community groups for ideas to develop awareness, as there is a considerable crossover in the strategies you are likely to use.

Ideas for involving national organisations in practical action and/or skills development

- See the sections on national businesses and local community groups for ideas to involve national organisations in practical action, as there is a considerable crossover in the strategies you are likely to use.

- If you are not sure where to start, focus on organisations which deal specifically with social mobility, and arrange to gain access to their resources, for inspiration and ideas in the first instance.

- As with any of the organisations with whom you build relationships, remember that they are staffed with people who can be very useful mentors to your students, as well as people who can supervise work experience. Your prime intention may be to work with these organisations to develop strategic programmes, but they will all have something very practical to offer as workplaces and a source of people and experience.

Universities (Sphere 4: the national community)

What is the school already doing to raise the awareness of universities about social and global mobility?	What is the school already doing to involve universities in practical action and/or skills development?
What does or should motivate universities to get more involved in developing the school's vision of social and global mobility?	What can universities contribute to the vision of developing social and global mobility?
How is the school engaging with universities (eg through personal relationships, professional relationships, through influence, through outreach, and/or through a network)?	To what extent is the school really engaged with universities? How could the school become better engaged with universities?

How can we find out more about universities' involvement with the school's vision for social and global mobility?

Universities – particularly older and more established universities – are often very complex organisations. They cover vast areas of research and teaching, and their interests are often very widespread. The governance arrangements of older universities especially can be convoluted; decision-making can be lengthy and spread amongst various different bodies, and the choices made by universities regarding what they choose to do can often be highly dependent on external factors such as regulatory requirements and available funding. It can therefore be difficult to access the inner workings of universities, and even more difficult to influence their engagement with schools.

It is worth, therefore, finding out which contacts with universities already exist in the school's wider network. You may have built up a solid relationship with, for example, a specific department at a local (but nationally significant) university over a period of years, but this is not the case for most schools; most schools will need to start the process of connecting with a university or universities from a much lower level of engagement. Ideas for reaching out, in order to begin discussions and start finding out what universities think about the possibility of engaging with schools and promoting their position as hubs of social and global mobility, include the following:

- Ask staff and parents if they have any connections with universities – perhaps they work at a university, or perhaps they know people who work there. There are likely to be several alumni of universities amongst your parent body, too. Explain what you are trying to do – to gain access to people with whom you can talk about the central role that schools can play in developing social and global mobility, and to engage the universities in supporting this. Do the staff or parents know anyone with whom it might be useful for the school to talk?

- If you have ever taken in trainee teachers from universities, to support them through their professional development, track down the contact details of the people you dealt with at the university.

- Do some online research about which departments of which universities nationally are particularly interested in social and global mobility. Look at the work they have produced, and the academics who are driving it. Can you identify anyone with whom you think you might be able to find a synergy in the direction you and they are taking in the field of social and global mobility?

When you have identified who to talk to at universities, and you have worked out your priorities around who you think you should contact, and in which university or universities – who and where is likely to prove most fruitful for you as you seek to strengthen your mission – then ideally you will seek to sit down together, in order to share ideas and work out together how best to move forward, and with whom. You will need to develop ideas and propositions if your thinking is to turn into action, and the best ideas will probably come out of your discussions as your relationship strengthens. Below, however, are some ideas to prompt your initial thinking.

Ideas for raising universities' awareness about social and global mobility

- See if someone from school can give a talk or lecture at the university – to students and/or staff – about the Powerful Schools Vision and how you are turning it into a reality. There may be various different audiences which you could address, including the wider public, perhaps as part of a panel at a lecture designed to make the work of the university more publically accessible. Talking about what you are doing, and sharing ideas openly, is often the best way to engage people in absorbing and assimilating the ideas into their perspectives on the world.

- If the university offers teacher training courses, see how you can get involved. Quite apart from all the mutual benefits that this brings, it is an opportunity to influence the direction of teacher training by spreading and sharing ideas about what you are doing in school to promote social and global mobility. Trainee teachers who come into your school will see this at first hand; you might also find opportunities to contribute directly to courses run by the university, including both initial teacher training and post-graduate courses in education – you could lecture on those courses, host school visits and contribute to journals.

- Whenever university students are welcomed into school, either as teacher trainees or in any of the potential roles suggested in the section below, make awareness of social and global mobility part of their introduction or induction process. Talk openly and widely about it – this way, the ideas will permeate and will be shared beyond the school.

- Offer the school as a place of research, where, for example, post-graduates or final year university students could explore the impact on social and global mobility of the various projects that the school is undertaking as part of its overall vision.

- Consider co-creating a module on social and global mobility for a course which the university already runs. This can be time-consuming and is probably not the first step you will take in order to raise awareness, but it would certainly extend the reach of the school and begin to cement the concept of Powerful Schools at the heart of the academic establishment. In time, the ideas developed have the potential to spread out into wider academic and policy circles.

Ideas for involving universities in practical action and/or skills development

- Create a mentoring programme to support school students in their personal development and in widening their horizons. University students are an obvious choice to act as mentors, but university staff too can act as mentors. This kind of programme has a dual benefit – the mentees grow and develop in their personal skills, while the mentors develop a greater awareness of the value of social and global mobility, and a stronger sense of their ability to be able to influence it. Distance is no object – university students can build a rapport with school students over Skype, for instance. This programme could be as informal or as formal as you decide – it will need a clear aim, of course, and some clear guidelines about what the purpose of the sessions is. Time spent working out a framework for interaction is time well spent.

- Create a work experience programme for university students to come into schools and contribute to the work of the school, with an especial focus on activity that promotes social and global mobility. This could include:

  - running or contributing to some of the other projects aimed at developing greater social and global mobility in which the school is involved (*eg* school student work experience, a talks and lecture series, personal development programmes *etc*).

  - developing new links for the school – *eg* with local charities, local businesses, international organisations *etc*.

  - collecting information on best practice in social and global mobility – a kind of mini-research project.

- Create an international work experience programme for university students and staff – any of the above tasks could just as easily be accomplished by students coming from abroad, who could work with the school as part of a university-sponsored programme for a period of a few weeks or even months. Many universities offer the opportunity for their students to live and work overseas during their course – part of the universities' own drive to develop greater social and global mobility – and it makes enormous sense to strengthen this by allowing the student to work in an environment which is also very focused on social and global mobility, and to contribute to it.

- Find opportunities for school students to visit the university or universities, to see what happens there, to learn to feel comfortable there, and to see what universities have to offer. Do your best to ensure that these opportunities are open to all, not just those students identified as (or who self-identify as) particularly academically able, or, conversely, to economically or personally disadvantaged students who might not otherwise consider university. All school students need to feel equally valued by the school: they all need to be able to access these opportunities to stretch their horizons.

- Consider developing courses and/or certificates with a university that can be run in school. These might range from courses which facilitate access to university (like university foundation courses), or courses which develop some of the higher order thinking skills that universities value, and which also prepare students to be more robust in life beyond school. A project like this might start more simply with, for example, an essay competition preceded by some training in school on how best to think and to structure ideas.

People of international influence (Sphere 5: the international community)

What is the school already doing to raise the awareness of people of international influence about social and global mobility?	What is the school already doing to involve people of international influence in practical action and/or skills development?
What does or should motivate people of international influence to get more involved in developing the school's vision of social and global mobility?	What can people of international influence contribute to the vision of developing social and global mobility?
How is the school engaging with people of international influence (eg through personal relationships, professional relationships, through influence, through outreach, and/or through a network)?	To what extent is the school really engaged with people of international influence? How could the school become better engaged with people of international influence?

How can we find out more about the involvement of people of international influence with the school's vision for social and global mobility?

In many cases, this self-evaluation will be a short one: not many schools are lucky enough to have the patronage of people with international influence, although some will. Do think carefully, though, about all of your networks, and don't be afraid to ask your stakeholders if they know people who can help you. If you can identify people with international influence in your school networks, then do not be afraid to approach them and ask them how they feel about promoting social and global mobility – you may find that this is one of the causes for which they have a particular passion.

Ideas for raising the awareness of people of international influence about social and global mobility

- Meet with them and talk with them.
- Share the evidence with them for the benefits of social and global mobility, and how schools really can make a difference.
- Show them what you are doing in school, the difference it is already making, and how you envisage it developing.

Ideas for involving people of international influence in practical action and/or skills development

The capacity of busy, well-connected, highly influential people to contribute to school activity – and what they can contribute – will be limited by a number of factors, including their time, their other priorities and (very probably) their sensitivities around how their engagement might be perceived – they may, for example, have limitations on what they can contribute for political or diplomatic reasons, or because they are associated with a certain brand which may not sit well with the school. However, if they are able and willing to contribute to the development of social and global mobility in your school and/or in schools more generally, this could include:

- Talking to students about their life and telling them the story of the paths they have taken.
- Acting as an ambassador for the vision in the media and with national and international governmental organisations.
- Spreading the word through their networks about the value of schools in developing social and global mobility, how they are achieving this, and why they should be supported.
- Potentially contributing financially to the funding of programmes in school such as work experience, mentoring, international connections *etc*, including funding the staffing of these programmes.

International governmental organisations (Sphere 5: the international community)

What is the school already doing to raise the awareness of international governmental organisations about social and global mobility?	What is the school already doing to involve international governmental organisations in practical action and/or skills development?
What does or should motivate international governmental organisations to get more involved in developing the school's vision of social and global mobility?	What can international governmental organisations contribute to the vision of developing social and global mobility?
How is the school engaging with international governmental organisations (eg through personal relationships, professional relationships, through influence, through outreach, and/or through a network)?	To what extent is the school really engaged with international governmental organisations? How could the school become better engaged with international governmental organisations?

How can we find out more about the involvement of international governmental organisations with the school's vision for social and global mobility?

The term 'international governmental organisations' covers a wide field, including organisations such as:

- the institutions of the European Union (including the Council of Europe and the European Commission);
- the departments and institutions of the United Nations, including UNESCO;
- numerous global government-supported organisations such as

the Organisation for Economic Co-operation and Development (OECD).

Other national governments and their departments can also be included in this section, because the work that is happening in different national contexts can also spark ideas and thoughts about social and global mobility. Be curious – do a broad-brush search to see what you can find out there. Use the Select Bibliography in this book as a starting point if you want, or just start looking. Set it, perhaps, as a research task for interested teachers or students – this is a good way to engage them more effectively. See what you can find and see what this sets you thinking about.

Social mobility – and global mobility – are not new concepts on the international stage. Much has been written about social mobility in particular (see the Select Bibliography), and it is embedded into the UN's Sustainable Development Goals. Remember, though, that these are only ideas – there is no template yet for schools, and even if such a template existed, school leaders should approach it cautiously, because, fundamentally, schools need to work with their children and in the context where they are situated. This does not mean that they should not expect their students to have the same access to opportunity – local, national and global – as students in other schools elsewhere in the world – on the contrary, in fact. It does mean, however – as school leaders know full well – that each school is unique, and demands its own unique approach, albeit to the same goal. Schools should never use difference as an excuse for lower achievements; although their task may be more challenging in a school with, for example, a lower socio-economic student profile, they cannot use this as an excuse not to pursue the goal of greater social and global mobility. On the whole, however, schools are driven to make a difference for their young people, and will go the extra mile to make it happen, coming up with endless creative solutions. These solutions need to be grounded in the specific situation of the school itself; reading the evidence gathered by international governmental organisations about social and global mobility in order to prompt your thinking will be interesting, will open your mind to possibility, and will reassure you that you are on the right track … ultimately, however, it is you and your school who will lead the way in your community, and will in turn provide practical inspiration for others.

Ideas for raising the awareness of international governmental organisations about social and global mobility

Across this documentation, there is a general acknowledgement that schools are key to enabling social mobility, largely because an education provides young people with more choices for their future. What you won't find, however, are many detailed and practical studies of how schools can lead this social drive – this is new territory, and as you develop the vision of a Powerful School in practice, bear in mind that at some stage it would be good for information about the practical programmes you put in place to be more widely noted, evaluated, verified and disseminated. This evidence will be particularly worth noting if it stems from a number of different sources – other Powerful Schools, ideally working in conjunction with one another. When you are ready for this, consider:

- working with an academic research team from one of your university partners to track and evaluate what you are doing.
- spreading the word about your success through your networks – keep the information flowing.
- write articles, give speeches, have conversations with people of influence … essentially, take every opportunity to raise awareness.

If what you are saying is interesting and practical – and especially if you can demonstrate that you really have been effective in enhancing social and global mobility – it will be passed on, and will have the potential at some stage, in some form, to attract the attention of, and influence, international governmental organisations, which can in turn redirect resources to developing the vision further and influence other national organisations to explore and adopt some of the ideas. None of this will happen overnight – it will take time to build the Powerful Schools Vision, and more time to spread the word about it. It is worth doing, though, because of the potential positive impact this could have on young people across the world.

Other ideas for involving international governmental organisations in practical action and/or skills development

- Internships and work experience placements in international governmental organisations are highly prized and normally reserved for young adults, but this does not mean that schools should not keep trying to find opportunities to add this kind of work experience to the school's portfolio.

- International study exchanges sponsored by international governmental organisations such as the EU Erasmus scheme are similarly extremely popular and usually aimed at young adults. Again, though, it is worth studying these schemes to see what elements could be replicated in a new scheme aimed at younger students.

International organisations, businesses, movements (Sphere 5: the international community)

What is the school already doing to raise the awareness of international organisations about social and global mobility?	What is the school already doing to involve international organisations in practical action and/or skills development?
What does or should motivate international organisations to get more involved in developing the school's vision of social and global mobility?	What can international organisations contribute to the vision of developing social and global mobility?
How is the school engaging with international organisations (eg through personal relationships, professional relationships, through influence, through outreach, and/or through a network)?	To what extent is the school really engaged with international organisations? How could the school become better engaged with international organisations?

How can we find out more about the involvement of international organisations with the school's vision for social and global mobility?

The term 'international organisation' is a very broad one, which encompasses a whole range of groups. Some of them are particularly pertinent to social and global mobility, including:

- Research-led organisations which can often influence international social or educational policy, such as McKinsey, the Boston Consulting Group and the Brookings Institute.
- Charities which work in a number of countries.
- Organisations with an educational focus such as the English Speaking Union.

- Global businesses, which often have significant funds at their disposal and sometimes their own charitable foundations.

In practice, however, any organisation with an international dimension has the potential to create an impact in the international arena, and to support schools and school systems. Some international organisations will prefer to focus on local impact – single communities, perhaps – and others will prefer to have a more wide-reaching (but less personal) impact, *eg* on educational or social projects which affect hundreds or thousands of people. Many national organisations have an international dimension, and from the perspective of a single school it is probably wise to base any international outreach on a firm national base first, reaching through the national organisations with whom you are connected in order to reach the international. After all, you want to focus your activity where it is most likely to be effective from the outset, and while this does not necessarily mean that you should begin small, it is probable that unless you are connected personally with people with international influence, then the international dimension of your influence is likely to happen at a later stage, and will arise in conjunction with the work of several other schools.

Ideas for raising the awareness of international organisations about social and global mobility

- If you are highly successful, highly influential and very well-connected, and you also lead the way in developing effective programmes that lead towards greater social and global mobility, then you may well attract the attention of international organisations, and you may even find yourself the subject of a case study or other research. It is more likely that you will start to reach out and connect internationally with other schools, and they will in turn connect with their national organisations, as also included within this group are any organisations which may be national organisations, but which are based in countries other than your own. Look again at the sections of this chapter which deal with national organisations, universities, national government and national businesses: they will give you ideas which you can share with your counterparts abroad, and help you both to develop, together, further strategies for building relationships that will lead to action that in turn will enhance the powerful effect of the network in ensuring that schools lead the drive towards greater social and global mobility.

Ideas for involving international organisations in practical action and/or skills development

- Look for opportunities for your students to engage in any or all of the following activities, commonly run by international organisations:
  - competitions;
  - sponsorship – *eg* travel awards;
  - internships.
- Don't forget, whenever you are in contact with any organisation, wherever it is based, to explore how your students can benefit from contact with staff in these organisations. Opportunities for work experience and skills development programmes should always be high on your agenda.

Other schools and school-to-school networks (Spheres 3, 4 and 5: the local, national and global community)

What is the school already doing to raise the awareness of other schools about social and global mobility?	What is the school already doing to involve other schools in practical action and/or skills development?
What does or should motivate other schools to get more involved in developing the school's vision of social and global mobility?	What can other schools contribute to the vision of developing social and global mobility?
How is the school engaging with other schools (eg through personal relationships, professional relationships, through influence, through outreach, and/or through a network)?	To what extent is the school really engaged with other schools? How could the school become better engaged with other schools?

How can we find out more about the involvement of other schools with the school's vision for social and global mobility?

Schools belong to many different networks of schools, from local networks to professional associations and international organisations. These networks provide channels of communication – both formal and informal – for you to ask what other schools are doing to develop a concerted strategy focused on social and global mobility, and to share good practice. If you have conducted a thorough initial audit, this will also provide you with a good starting point for an understanding of how connected you are in practice with other schools. You may have to delve deeper into your stakeholder communities, however, to find out about other personal connections, and connections that, for example, local community groups have with other schools, all of which are good starting points for developing further action. Keep asking your stakeholders the question about links that they have with other schools, and you will build up an even better picture of how deeply interconnected you are with other schools. The more solid your relationships with other schools, the easier it will be to ask what they are doing, and to share what you are doing.

Ideas for raising the awareness of other schools about social and global mobility

- Make a policy decision to play a full part in initiatives promoted by national government to encourage employability and/or social mobility, and/or any programmes which will develop the personal skills (confidence *etc*) that young people need to become socially and globally mobile. By engaging with enthusiasm in these initiatives – of which there are, encouragingly, increasing numbers – you will benefit from the accumulated wisdom of others, and potentially even access to funding streams, and you will also develop an ever stronger network and platform to be able to share what you are doing in school.

- Look for opportunities to share insights about what you are doing with your colleagues from other schools. Host networking meetings and cluster groups at your school, in order to make it easier to connect your staff with staff from other schools, and use the occasion – no matter what the main topic of discussion was intended to be – to highlight your progress towards developing greater social and global mobility; make sure all staff who go out to other schools are fully equipped with knowledge about what you are doing in school, and are fired up to share it with passion. Talking with staff from other schools is a precursor to inviting representatives from other schools to come and see what you are doing, and to replicate and extend the process in their school. The more schools who are engaged in actively increasing more comprehensive and focused opportunities for students to develop the skills they need to become more socially and globally mobile, the more new ideas will emerge about how to do this effectively, from which all schools can benefit.

Ideas for involving other schools in practical action and/or skills development

- Build your networks of schools. Reach out to other schools to encourage them to join you in programmes where you are already working with other schools, and/or where you know you would benefit from greater involvement from other schools. Be generous in sharing your knowledge and insights: overcome the competitiveness which exists between schools but which undermines collaboration and the fundamental power that schools can have to effect change when they work together. The more schools who are involved in actively developing opportunities for students, and building networks with their stakeholders, the more powerful their overall effect. This is key to the Powerful Schools Vision: all schools working to drive social and global mobility in society, recognised and assisted by their stakeholders, who collectively represent the rest of society more generally. Simply by understanding their potential power, and by sharing this understanding with their community and stakeholders, schools can make an active difference, because high expectations, clearly articulated, are one of the key drivers of ambitious change. Knowledge is power; shared knowledge is more powerful still, and the more schools which are involved in pursuing this shared vision, the more effective it will be.
- Co-ordinate with other schools on programmes where you have shared stakeholders; anything at national and international level, and possibly even at local level too, depending on where the schools are located. This could include;
  - Work experience programmes (including work-shadowing) – if schools can share their contacts and work together to ask these stakeholders to expand opportunities for work experience, this will enrich the programmes for the students. It also sends the message to businesses (and others) that schools can work effectively together as powerful drivers of social activity, and are not just individual entities for whom the business is somehow doing a favour.
  - International programmes, including trips and visits.

Simply sharing experience of what works, and how to overcome hurdles, can be very useful to schools as they set up their own programmes and learn from the successes and mistakes of others. Working together to develop more programmes, and to involve more students in existing partnerships, can also be hugely beneficial – it shares the workload, it increases the capacity for creative thought and, consequently, creative solutions (especially how to make trips more affordable), and it can make programmes more viable financially because of the higher numbers involved.

- Programmes involving universities and/or further education partners; these partners are often much larger than a single school, and are motivated too by the power of outreach to as wide a group of young people as possible. Working with a network of schools is often more attractive to them than working with just one school.

- Encourage all the schools with which you are connected to audit what they are doing, and to share the results with the other schools in your networks. See what ideas emerge, and think about how to share these ideas with others so that they translate into more action.

Chapter 8

Bringing it all together – what do you do next?

This book set out to be a tool to help school leaders focus their existing thoughts on social and global mobility into a cohesive understanding of the power of schools to make a difference. Each school will take a slightly different path, responding to its specific circumstances and needs, but when several schools – all schools – engage actively with the vision of Powerful Schools outlined in the previous chapters, the potential for change is enormous.

Change happens because people take action, and schools are well-used to leading the way in taking action. Drawing on the ideas and activities in this book, schools will hopefully have a better understanding of what they can do, and a clearer pathway forward.

As a school leader or teacher who has read this book, what you will now have is:

- an understanding of how to discover what you already do in school to develop opportunities for greater social and global mobility;
- an understanding of who your stakeholders are;

- ideas about how to engage your stakeholders and what you might put into practice in school.

What you now need to do is to:

- work out where to start and with whom to start;
- work out how much time and effort you want to devote to this;
- make a start.

Sometimes the only way to make things happen is just to do them. Social and global mobility matter enormously, and schools are in many ways best placed to turn them into even more of a reality for young people, now and in the future.

If just one teacher or school leader, however, finds just one single suggestion in this book that prompts them to give just one child a greater opportunity to become more socially and globally mobile, then it will have been worth it. Anything else is a bonus – and the winners will be not only our young people, but all of us.

Why not begin tomorrow?

Select Bibliography: useful sources of further reading

A Family Affair: Intergenerational Social Mobility across OECD Countries. OECD. 2010 www.oecd.org/eco/public-finance/chapter%205%20gfg%202010.pdf

Career Education: A World of Possibilities. National Parent Forum of Scotland. Edinburgh: 2016. www.npfs.org.uk/wp-content/uploads/2015/09/NPFS_world_of_possibilities_1509_E.pdf

Cracking the code: how schools can improve social mobility. Child Poverty and Social Mobility Commission. London, 2014. ISBN: 978-1-78105-410-9. www.educationengland.org.uk/documents/pdfs/2014-soc-mob-child-pov.pdf

Developing the Young Workforce: Scotland's Youth Employment Strategy; Implementing the Recommendations of the Commission for Developing Scotland's Young Workforce. The Scottish Government. Edinburgh, 2014. ISBN: 978-1-78544-033-5. www.gov.scot/Resource/0046/00466386.pdf

Dismantling the Barriers to Social Mobility. Gaffney, D & Baumberg, B. TUC. London, 2014. www.tuc.org.uk/sites/default/files/Social_Mobility_Touchstone_Extra.pdf

Inequality of opportunity, income inequality and economic mobility: Some international comparisons. Brunori P, Ferreira F & Peragine V. World Bank. 2011. documents.worldbank.org/curated/en/2013/01/17150436/inequality-opportunity-income-inequality-economic-mobility-some-international-comparisons

Inequality Matters. UN Department of Social and Economic Affairs. New York, 2013. ISBN: 978-92-1-130322-3. www.un.org/esa/socdev/documents/reports/InequalityMatters.pdf

Opening Doors, Breaking Barriers: A Strategy for Social Mobility. The Cabinet Office. London, 2011. www.gov.uk/government/uploads/system/uploads/attachment_data/file/61964/opening-doors-breaking-barriers.pdf

Smart moves. A new approach to international assignments and global mobility. Deloitte. 2010. www2.deloitte.com/content/dam/Deloitte/us/Documents/Tax/us-tax-talent-smartmoves-062410.pdf

The Mobility Manifesto. A report on cost-effective ways to achieve greater social mobility through education, based on work by the Boston Consulting Group. The Sutton Trust. London, 2010. www.suttontrust.com/wp-content/uploads/2010/03/120100312_mobility_manifesto2010.pdf

Useful websites

Barclays Life Skills. www.barclayslifeskills.com

Boston Consulting Group. Perspectives. www.bcgperspectives.com

Brookings Institute. www.brookings.edu/research/topics/education

Careers New Zealand. www.careers.govt.nz

Duke of Edinburgh Award Scheme. www.dofe.org

English Speaking Union. www.esu.org

Hour of Code. code.org/learn

Lego League. www.firstlegoleague.org

McKinsey & Company. www.mckinsey.com/insights

Model United Nations. en.wikipedia.org/wiki/Model_United_Nations

My future. Career Insights. myfuture.edu.au/career-insight?pi=1

National Careers Service, England and Wales. nationalcareersservice.direct.gov.uk/Pages/Home.aspx

Sutton Trust. www.suttontrust.com

Young Enterprise. www.young-enterprise.org.uk